2310049 FRAME, Janet
The envoy from Mirror City
Vol.3.
8.95

B/FRA

-0. MAY 1986

0 7043 2875 5

Please renew/return this item by the last date shown.

So that your telephone call is charged at local rate,
please call the numbers as set out below:

	From Area codes 01923 or 0208:	From the rest of Herts:
Renewals:	01923 471373	01438 737373
Enquiries:	01923 471333	01438 737333
Minicom:	01923 471599	01438 737599

L32b

18 JUN 1988

31 DEC 1988

22/7/00

-8 JUN 1991

2 2 AUG 2003

25 JAN 1992

22 FEB 1992

29 FEB 1992

2 4 AUG 2004

21 MAR 1992

11 APR 1992

2 6 OCT 2007

2 6 JAN 1995

1 0 JAN 1998

L 33

The Women's Press Ltd
124 Shoreditch High Street, London E1

Janet Frame   Photo by Anne Noble

Janet Frame was born in Dunedin, New Zealand, in 1924. Her works include ten novels, among them *Owls Do Cry* (The Women's Press, 1985), *State of Siege, Scented Gardens for the Blind* (The Women's Press, 1982), *Yellow Flowers in the Antipodean Room, Faces in the Water* (The Women's Press, 1980) and *Living in the Maniototo* (The Women's Press, 1981), which won the Fiction Prize, New Zealand Book Awards, 1980. She has also published four collections of stories and sketches, one of which, *You Are Now Entering The Human Heart*, was published by The Women's Press in 1984; a volume of poetry and a children's book, *Mona Minim and the Smell of the Sun*.

Janet Frame is New Zealand's most distinguished living novelist, and she has won a number of distinctions in her native country. The first volume of her autobiography, *To the Is-Land*, won the James Wattie Book of the Year Award in 1983; and the second volume, *An Angel at my Table*, won the New Zealand Literature Award for Non-Fiction in 1984. In 1983 she was given a CBE in the Queen's Birthday Honours List.

Janet Frame

The Envoy from Mirror City

An Autobiography: Volume 3

The Women's Press

First published in Great Britain by
The Women's Press Limited 1985
A member of the Namara Group
124 Shoreditch High Street, London E1 6JE

First published by Hutchinson Group (NZ) Limited 1984
32-34 View Road, Glenfield, Auckland 10, New Zealand

British Library Cataloguing in Publication Data

Frame, Janet
    The Envoy from Mirror City: an autobiography:
    volume 3.
    1. Frame, Janet — Biography 2. Authors, New
    Zealand — 20th century — Biography
    I. Title
    823   PR9639.3.F72/

ISBN 0-7043-2875-5

Printed and bound in Great Britain
by Nene Litho and Woolnough Bookbinding
both of Wellingborough, Northants

This third volume
is dedicated to my friends and family,
whom I've mentioned, and in particular to
Professor Robert Hugh Cawley and his colleagues.

Acknowledgements

Grateful thanks to John Money (John Forrest) of Baltimore, Maryland, John and Rose Marie Beston of Pittsford, New York, and Bill Brown and Paul Wonner of San Francisco, for the hospitality that enabled me to complete my manuscript.

Extract from 'In Memory of W. B. Yeats' from W. H. Auden: Collected Poems, edited by Edward Mendelson reprinted by permission of Random House Inc., New York, and Faber and Faber, Publishers, London.

Extracts from 'Notebooks' by Albert Camus translated from the French by Philip Thody reprinted by permission of Hamish Hamilton Ltd., London, and Alfred A. Knopf, Inc., New York. French edition copyright Editions Gallimard 1962.

Extract from 'On No Work of Words' from Collected Poems 1934-52 by Dylan Thomas reprinted by permission of J. M. Dent and Sons Ltd., London, and the literary executors of the Dylan Thomas Estate.

Index of Chapters

Part Two   At Home in the City

Part One

Triple Witness

Earthless,
the
Sailing

1

Far from the New Zealand coast the *Ruahine* pitched and rolled through the wintry July seas.

The six-berth inside cabin had none of the spaciousness pictured in the tourist brochures: there was scarcely room to move, while only the privileged faces of the women in the top end bunks could receive the air (warm, stale) churned in by the cream-coloured 'blower' or ventilator angled from the ceiling. Isolated from sky, earth, light in a rich element of time, I lay on my lower bunk by the cabin door and listened to the excited voices of my fellow-passengers — two office girls from Hamilton making their first visit overseas; a dark-haired small woman from Australia who had been 'around the world' several times and was eager to display photographs taken on her travels; a schoolteacher returning to the Midlands after a year's visit on exchange to New Zealand; a quiet middle aged woman, the daughter of a famous Norwegian writer, and herself a writer, returning home to Norway. In the sickeningly warm, throbbing cabin where even the walls seemed to surge and sway, in the claustrophobic atmosphere of bodies stacked as if on shelves, of the odours and shadows of the draped newly-washed or dry underwear and stockings, limp disembodied legs over every railing, in the swarm of words circling a frantic excitement of anticipation and anxiety, my head whirled while my stomach heaved with every roll and pitch and plunge of the *Ruahine*. The discomfort could be eased neither by the Kwells tablets recommended by Jess Whitworth, a seasoned traveller and friend of Frank Sargeson, nor by the lavender-perfumed, lavender-ribboned smelling salts in their heart-shaped cut-glass bottle. Unable to eat meals, I ate water biscuits that Jess had given to me with the assurance that I would come to look on them as my 'best friends'.

After three days of continuing seasickness and a return of a recent attack of 'flu, I was taken to the ship's hospital where, in a state of great weakness familiar to those who ever have suffered from motion sickness I lay almost helpless for nearly two weeks until as the ship began to slow down preparing to enter the Panama Canal, I was able to sit in a chair and watch the theatre of the Panamanian jungle with its basking crocodiles; the gaudy parrots flitting among the trees that leaned, burdened with blossoming vines, to touch the water; to the accompaniment of the American guide announcing the dollar worth of everything within sight. By the time the ship reached Curaçao, and the engines and the movement ceased as we anchored for the day in Willemstad, my sickness had gone, and with the ship unmoving except for a gentle swaying, I was able to eat the buffet lunch, and to go ashore at Willemstad, my first landfall in a foreign country. How clearly I understood the travellers' custom at the end of a long voyage of stooping to kiss the earth! In Willemstad however, the immediate earth was concrete, and the smell was not of fresh grass but of oil from the refinery, yet the light was new, otherworldly above and upon the dull reds, browns, cream of the buildings, and the foliage glittered paintbox green with a poisonous brightness. I wandered alone through the streets of Willemstad. I sat in the Museum grounds watching unfamiliar lizards basking on unfamiliar stones, and birds that I'd never seen before or heard singing, flocking in the trees. Then I walked by the river and, noting the empty bottles and tins, I was aware of the 'other country' comparison — were not our rivers pure and swift, not sluggish and polluted? And the people walking by the river, how poor they seemed to be, and sickly, unlike the robust New Zealanders! A small travelling zoo had set up its Sunday entertainment on a plot of waste land: cramped cages housing a miserable fur-patched bear and a stinking brown-yellow lion, each confirming my opinion, acquired in New Zealand, that people 'overseas' had little compassion for animals, also that overseas was poor, not as civilized as New Zealand.. In my first foreign country I still wore the old clothes of prejudice. I'd also seen for the first time a group of people whose skin was not shades of brown or yellow but dusky black. At school I had been taught that Maori and Pakeha had equal opportunities and I believed what I had been taught. I had also learned that Chinese people excelled in gardening and fruit-growing, the Greeks were excellent fishermen, while the Maoris were the best drivers of heavy vehicles.

'Maoris are very mechanically minded,' a lecturer at Training College had told us, a class of Pakehas. Now, faced with Afro-Americans and Indians I dismissed from my mind the comparison with teams of slaves. I said 'Hello', heartily, to show my lack of prejudice but I became alarmed when my greeting was followed by an attempt at conversation, for I had nothing to say. And here I was, travelling overseas to 'broaden my experience' and already undergoing the change forced on every new traveller and accomplished by examining not the place of arrival but the place of departure. The years of cowboy films, of white-horsed fairhaired 'goodies', and dark-skinned dark-horsed and hatted 'baddies', the Mexican bandits and rustlers against the honest hardworking American ranchers, the American Indians intent on destruction and massacre while the cowboys and cavalry sought 'peace and a fair deal for all', these films seen in childhood, all goodie-baddie drama including detective drama, while letting reason function, had stored feelings that lay undisturbed, perhaps unknown and unsuspected, but ready to overcome the guardian reason to try to direct the unwary traveller in the new land.

Before I returned over the Willemstad pontoon bridge to the *Ruahine* I performed a ritual that also had its origin in what I had heard or read or thought in New Zealand where, it seemed, everyone had been singing

> *Drinking rum and Coca Cola*
> *Waiting for the Yankee dollar . . .*

The American guide through the Panama Canal had used the word 'dollar' in almost every sentence: here, in Willemstad, advertisements for Coca Cola were everywhere. I completed my first visit to a foreign land by drinking my first bottle of Coca Cola with as much reverence as if I were sipping wine in Church. One needs to be reminded that in the late nineteen fifties Coca Cola had an aura of magic, of promise, as a symbol to many outside the United States of America of all that was essentially American, generous, good, dollar-flavoured, new-world, bathed in the glow of a country's morning that was not yet tarnished by the scrutiny of daylight.

For the final week of my journey, still unable to visit the dining room once the ship had begun to sail, I took my bedding on deck and slept in the cool air beneath the sky returning only when the early morning deck-scrubbers began sloshing their buckets of water. Much had happened on board during my stay in the hospital: the mixture of passengers had swirled to form new compounds: the comics, the leaders, the gossip targets, the wonderful and the beautiful, like viruses, had been isolated, identified and studied. The enterprising Pacific and now the Atlantic were not so busy with their own drifting of objects on distant shores that they had not been able to cast upon the decks of the *Ruahine* these special passengers that rise to the surface on every long voyage. Much talked about and admired in our cabin was the beautiful brilliant blonde scholarship winner on her way to Oxford; she was envied, too, for her many escorts, her dinners at the captain's table, her dances with the ship's doctor, while the others, like the 'others' on land or sea, had to be content with partners of lesser glory. There was also the young pianist who surrounded by admirers, practised confidently in the lounge. Oh how I longed to be admired for any accomplishments I might have! Oh how I longed for everyone to know that I was travelling overseas on a literary grant! How could everyone appear to be so self-assured? And there were the two office girls with their store of purchases from Panama and Willemstad (everyone except the Norwegian writer and I had bought silk kimonos, pyjamas, scarves, glittering purses), why they talked and behaved as if they owned the world and as soon as they set foot in Great Britain the ownership papers would be handed to them at a special ceremony. Perhaps the Australian woman with her photographs and her tales of travel was not as confident as she appeared for the more she talked, the more I began to compare her with a character who has been set in motion and is unable to stop, for she had been to and fro, to and fro, from north to south and east to west and there was occasionally panic in her eyes when someone asked where she planned to live 'finally' 'in the end', for, obviously, she couldn't travel for ever . . . or could she? Sometimes she appeared to feel that she had no choice, it was too late to turn back, there was now no 'back' to turn to. I wondered, briefly, what if I became like her, a doomed traveller with no feeling of home?

As I watched and listened I comforted myself by trying to feel superior as I said to myself, 'Little do they know that I'm recording everything in my mind, that I can see through them, beneath their masks, right to the bottom of their heart, for if I'm to be and stay a writer I must follow all the signs in everything they say and do, and in the silence and inactivity, reading their face and the faces and the eyes that are mapped with their private isobars and isotherms above the fertile lands, the swamps secret with marsh birds, the remote mountains sharp with rock formations, softened with snow. I must forever watch and listen.

That voyage has not stayed in my mind in complete detail. I remember only the nightmare and the envious longings. I remember the day in Willemstad, the groupings of the passengers, their excitement and anticipation. I remember the serious doctor who advised me never again to travel by sea. I remember the red-faced captain with gold braid encircling him or seeming to as if it were markings on a teapot — these details stay like small ships tossed on my own waves of seasickness where as those who have suffered this will know, the abiding dream is for the ship to stop moving, for the sick passenger to be put ashore at some island, any island, any land that happens by as if land ever happened by in search of a lone castaway. In the past I had practised endurance. During the voyage I had not been prepared, I was unable to organize my defence against the awful diminishing of my human power where every move was a nauseating effort and the seconds, the minutes, the hours, the days became a mountain of oppressive time. The reward of surviving the crossing of the Pacific became the vision of the gradual melting of the terrible mountain until the final handful of rock and earth was buried by the looming Destination.

After thirty-two days at sea, on the day after my thirty-second birthday, the *Ruahine* berthed at Southampton where the passengers boarded the waiting train to Waterloo Station, London.

The
Gentleman

2

Waterloo Station. I am standing with my two suitcases, my green haversack containing my typewriter, and I'm holding fast to my *Traveller's Joy* handbag as I propel my luggage towards the street and the row of taxis. Repeating almost dutifully to myself, 'so this is London,' I watch as the other passengers are swept away by welcoming groups of friends and relatives. It's raining and grey and the black taxis are like hearses. With a sense of sweet satisfaction in knowing that soon I shall be safe in a room in the Friends' Hostel, and able to claim at last a bed on earth, I hail a taxi (as I have seen it done on films) and say boldly, 'The Friends' Hostel in Euston Road, please.'

The taxi sways sickeningly up and down rainsplashed streets to Euston Road and the Society of Friends' Hostel. And here I stand, my luggage on the footpath beside me, outside the building that will be my home for at least a week. Overtaken by the joy of having arrived at last, I herd my luggage closer to me as I climb the steps to the front door and press the bell. Footsteps. The door opens.

'I'm Janet Frame from New Zealand,' I say quickly to the grey-haired woman. 'I wrote to you, reserving a room for a week.'

The woman frowned. 'Your name again?'

'Janet Frame, from New Zealand.' I emphasize *New Zealand*.

'Will you wait one moment, please.'

The woman studies a book at the reception desk and returns, frowning more deeply.

'There's been a mistake. We have received no letter from a Janet Frame in New Zealand. We are fully booked. It's the end of August, you know.'

'Oh yes.' I think, 'Of course I know, all those books with descriptions of Bank Holidays. "August for the people and their favourite islands." '

The woman repeats, 'I'm sorry. There are no vacancies. Your letter did not reach us.'

Disbelieving, fighting off panic, I play what I think must be my winning card.

'I've a friend in New Zealand who *always* stays with you. Jess Whitworth.' (Surely she remembers Jess Whitworth!)

'I'm sorry, Miss Frame. I don't recall her. And we are fully booked. Perhaps next week . . . '

I'm near tears now.

'But next week's too late. I'm *all the way from New Zealand*. I'm just off the boat.'

The woman smiles patiently.

'We have guests coming from all over the world. Every day.'

'But I did write to you. And I'm just off the boat. I've never been to London before,' I add bleakly. 'I've never been to London before, and I don't know where to stay.'

I can still see myself surrounded by my remnants of New Zealand — the two old suitcases, the green canvas haversack that Frank Sargeson had insisted I would need because thirty years earlier he had carried a haversack on his walking tour of Europe, the leather Traveller's Joy handbag costing an enormous ten pounds that had been the gift from the Gordon family. As I stood uncertainly at the door of the hostel, I remembered how Frank and I had pored over his old yellowed copies of the *New Statesman*, reading the advertisements on the back page — Rooms to Let: St John's Wood, Swiss Cottage, Hampstead Heath, Earls Court — names then unknown, romantically enticing, but now seeming like stark cliff faces without hand or foothold, inhospitably plunging me into the dark unknown.

'You have no friends in London?' the woman asked.

'No,' I quavered.

'There's the YWCA Hostel not far from here. I'll phone and see if they have a room.'

Minutes later she returned with the welcome news that there was a 'share room' vacant for two nights.

The woman offered to ring for a taxi.

'Please. And thank you.'

Standing with my luggage on the grimy London steps I felt fleetingly at the back of my mind the perennial drama of the Arrival and its place in myth and fiction, and I again experienced the thrilling sense of being myself excavated as reality, the ore of the polished fiction. The journey, the arrival, the surprises and problems of arrival. And even in my first experience in London there'd been also the reminder of the *Letter* in fiction — the missing letter, the discovered letter, the letter of such portent that lives are lost and destinies changed as in Macbeth's 'They met me in the day of success; and I have learned by the perfectest report, they have more in them than mortal knowledge . . . ' and the role of the bearer of the letter, of the successful or failed messenger. For a moment the loss of the letter I had written seemed to be unimportant beside the fictional gift of the loss as if within every event lay a reflection reached only through the imagination and its various servant languages, as if, like the shadows in Plato's cave, our lives and the world contain mirror cities revealed to us by our imagination, the Envoy.

In spite of fictional possibilities and enthusiasms, that first day in London was dreary and uncomfortable. Already, in late August, London was drawing down the blinds for a darkening winter. The YWCA where I found a room for two nights reminded me of a mental hospital without the noise, without the constant jingling of keys and the attempt to control the guests, although there were efforts at control in the sheet of rules pinned inside the doors of the bedrooms and bathrooms and lavatories that were in rows, institutional in appearance and smell. The baths were cavernous, the floors were set with chilling black and white tiles.

Please leave the bath as you would wish others to find it. A suitable hostel translation of the Golden Rule, sensibly moral and assuming altruism and the practice of Christian principles. The office downstairs held a cage where luggage could be left. A stern-faced woman supervised the entrance and exit of guests and distributed mail as if the letters were holy tablets, and, aware of the power of letters, I know they may have been.

10

Although I found the YWCA intimidating with its continued presence of authority, I observed that the guests were happy, friendly; there was an atmosphere of excitement as arrivals, departures, excursions were discussed. The cafeteria food was cheap and plentiful and I quickly became one of the group of excited 'strangers to London'. I shared my room with a woman from Singapore who, as innocent as I, dreaming of visiting Piccadilly Circus, travelled there by Underground and not only discovered the truth of Piccadilly Circus (that it was not, as we believed, a real circus) but spent the day trapped in the Underground.

I marvelled at my freedom, especially as the Victorian atmosphere and appearance of many of the London buildings had released a fountain (of fear) from my recent past. My drenching was temporary: again the contemplation of the parallel, the mirror dream, sustained me, proofed me against the nightmare of the past.

On my first evening I telephoned the address in Clapham Common where Jess Whitworth had stayed in the Garden Room. In spite of disillusionment with the reality of romantic names, I still hoped for a pleasant stay in a *Garden Room* that would be as I dreamed, and when a Patrick Reilly, one of the tenants of the main house, explained that he was in charge while the owners were in Scotland, and that a Garden Room was vacant for seventeen and six a week and that I could move in any time, I forgot the many miseries of my arrival in London and began to look forward to a measure of paradise.

I could move in the next day, Patrick Reilly suggested. He'd have a day off work and could meet me and see me settled in the room. How kind of him, I thought.

The down-under accent, he said, had proved I was a genuine enquirer.

My departure from the YWCA was made through the ritual of censure because I had undertaken to stay two nights.

'Rooms are hard to get at this time of year. Refunds are not usual,' the warden said.

I accepted the necessary underlining of my imperfect behaviour and lack of forethought. I apologized. I understood how institutions thrive on accuracy of moral edicts and on judgments which must be made as plain as the credit and debit of those who use the institutions.

The next afternoon I arrived by taxi at Cedars Road, Clapham Common North Side, to find Patrick Reilly waiting to escort me to my Garden Room.

And here was Mr Reilly carrying my luggage through the side gate to Garden Room Number Three. There were four rooms set in a row against a tall brick boundary wall, facing towards the back garden of the main house. They appeared to be shacks rather than rooms, with their floors set directly upon the earth with no damp course between.

'I hope you won't be in this room for the winter,' Patrick Reilly said. 'A woman died of pneumonia here last winter.'

He pointed to the end room.

'There's a Russian ballet dancer there now. And we had a European Prince last year.'

Patrick Reilly was talkative with a pleasant Irish accent. He was sturdily built, not tall, with greying hair, a large smooth pale face and brown well-spring eyes. His occasionally tightly pursed lips gave me a sign of a certain restriction of inward horizons: setting the limits, as it were. His step was agile and sure. He thrust the key into the lock of Number Three and with some urging and pushing he opened the door into a small damp-smelling room containing a narrow bed with some bedding, a curtained wardrobe, a chair, and on the rush-mat-covered floor a single electric plate connected to an electric meter, fed with shillings, just inside the door. There was one small square window by the door and one light suspended from the ceiling. A pile of assorted dishes and pots and pans stood on a box beside the electric ring.

'I need a place for my typewriter,' I said.

'I'll fetch a table from the cellar. It's full of old furniture and junk. And I'll show you the bathroom and the geyser in the main house. Like a cup of tea?'

And so I then inspected the cramped bathroom and tried to absorb Patrick Reilly's instructions on the working of the geyser that heated the bathwater. He warned me to be careful, or the geyser might explode. Someone had been killed, he said, a year or two earlier. And the house was almost wrecked.

'They were injured, anyway,' he corrected. 'It happened before my time.'

Patrick Reilly was beginning to acquire mythical attributes as The Greeter who was also The Warner: even during this first meeting he began to list the lurking dangers of Cedars Road, Clapham Common North Side. I supposed that he would deal later with London and the World.

He took me to his room next to the bathroom in the main house and I sat silently watching while he filled a kettle from the tap on the landing and lighting a gas ring on the table, boiled the water for a cup of tea. I knew I was seeing for the first time the ritual of a way of living that was new to me, where people lived alone in one room of a large house of many rooms, each self-contained except for the shared bathroom and lavatory and the water tap above the basin on the landing where Patrick had filled the kettle for our tea. Already I had noticed two men with buckets fetching their supply of water either for washing or for drinking.

'Women are not popular with landladies,' Patrick explained. 'They leave hair in the bathroom and are always washing clothes.'

He set two cups and saucers at one end of the large oilcloth-covered table, and lifting a full bottle of milk from a basin of water and grasping the bottle at both ends he gently rocked the milk to and fro, then lay it sideways on the table beside the cups and saucers.

'Bluetop. Jersey Island milk. I buy the best,' he said. 'That's how you spread the cream.'

He made the tea.

'I wait five minutes, no more, no less for the infusion.'

He said 'infusion' in a self-admiring way, like a surgeon who has diagnosed and will operate correctly.

He then probed apart the wrapping from a tube of biscuits, holding them for me to examine before he tipped three or four on to a plate.

'Digestive. Chocolate digestive. The dark kind.'

The tea was now brewed. I bit into my chocolate digestive and began to drink my tea.

'It's Tetley's Tips,' Patrick Reilly said. 'And the biscuits are Peek Frean.'

Peek Frean.

He spoke in a satisfied way as if he had achieved another point on the path to perfection.

I repeated the name. 'Peek Frean.' It fascinated me. I listened, marvelling, to Patrick Reilly's accent and the occasional Irish idiom that I knew from the Irish stereotype and from the Irish playwrights but had never heard spoken.

'I'm after going shopping,' he said. He appeared to be equally fascinated by my New Zealand accent. There was a bond between us, he said. Neither of us was English. He spoke with a dislike of

13

English. And as a colonial, he said, I would understand what the English had done to Ireland.

'They eat our pork and our butter and race our horses and we come here for jobs.'

The Republic of Ireland, he said, was God's Own Country and it was full of poverty. I thought, surprised, 'But isn't New Zealand God's Own Country?' It hadn't occurred to me that other countries, perhaps every country made this claim. In New Zealand, particularly among people who could see clearly, there had been jokes about our claim to be God's Own Country, and although I, too, had mocked the claim, I believed it since my childhood when I recited fervently the poetry of William Pember Reeves:

> *God girt her about with the surges*
>   *And winds of the masterless deep,*
> *Whose tumult uprouses and urges*
>   *Quick billows to sparkle and leap . . .*
>
> *Her never the fever-mist shrouding,*
>   *Nor drought of the desert may blight . . .*

So Ireland was God's Own Country, I said to myself, grasping this new fact of my overseas experience.

We finished our tea.

'If there's anything you want help with, just ask me,' Patrick Reilly said. 'You may call me Patrick.'

'Patrick. I'm Janet.'

He was impressed when I told him I was in England on a 'literary grant'.

'But I'm really on my way to the Balearic Islands . . . as soon as I can make arrangements here.'

'You're not going alone?'

'Oh yes.'

He frowned.

'You'll be in danger,' he warned. 'Foreign places are all dangerous. Even more than London.'

He was a member of the Catholic committee, he said, trying to rescue young Irish girls from prostitution. In his work as a bus driver he saw many such girls.

14

'They get into trouble,' he said sharply. 'I direct them to the Irish Hostels.'

He paused.

'And I'll look after you, Janet, while you're in London. But you mustn't go to Europe on your own. By the way, are you fancy free?'

'What an old-fashioned expression,' I thought. One that might have belonged to my mother's girlhood and not to Patrick Reilly who had said his age was forty-four.

'Oh yes, I'm fancy free.'

'Good. And think again about going abroad.'

'I must go,' I said.

'Writing isn't a very good occupation,' Patrick said.

'I once trained as a school teacher.'

'A school teacher! Now that's the sort of work you should be doing.'

He said excitedly that his sister was a school teacher in Ireland while his cousin was Archbishop of a northern town. Also, the woman who had once been his sweetheart had been a school teacher.

'M. stole her from me,' Patrick said. M. was an Irish correspondent much in the news in the late nineteen fifties.

A person's belief, with its implication of possession and ownership, that others could be 'stolen' from him, interested me as it had in New Zealand when Paula Lincoln accused a neighbour of 'stealing' her friends. Yet such facts of ownership are written into the legal description of 'enticement' where 'enticement' is a misdemeanor against property, the property here being a person 'owned' by another. Patrick did not explain particulars of the robbery that had left him without a fiancée.

As I was leaving the bedsitter he again warned me.

'Watch out for the blacks in London. They're everywhere. They're stealing all the work. Clapham's full of them.'

He drew his lips back from his gums and bared his teeth in an apparently unconscious gesture. I was repelled. I wanted to love the World and everyone in it ('the fullness thereof, the World and they that dwell therein . . . ').

Feeling insulted on behalf of those referred to as 'black', I said carefully, 'You mean the people from the West Indies and Africa?'

'Yes, the blacks.'

'I don't think people should be referred to by the colour of their skin,' I said anxiously.

'They're lower than us. They're the blacks,' he said almost viciously.

I let the new unpleasantness wash over me. He was ignorant, I decided. He didn't know and he didn't understand. Also, he was afraid. Nothing would make him change his mind while he was afraid.

'See you tomorrow,' he called as I went down the stairs.

'Yes,' I said, echoing, 'see you tomorrow,' realizing that for weeks I had been in a world where no-one said, 'See you tomorrow.'

I was grateful to Patrick Reilly. He was a natural helper. He was also dependable, self-satisfied, bigoted, lonely, religious with an endearing Irish accent. In spite of his largely disqualifying prejudice he was what my mother would have called 'a gentleman'. He was my first friend in London.

Keats and the Storytellers of Battersea

3

The reader may laugh at what I, in all my naiveté, imagined I would find when I boarded the bus number 137 to *Crystal Palace*. During those early weeks in keenest anticipation, I made other long bus journeys to places with haunting names — Ponders End, High Wycombe, Mortlake, Shepherds Bush, Swiss Cottage, each time arriving at a cluster of dreary-looking buildings set in a waste of concrete and brick and full of people who appeared to be pale, worried and smaller in build than most New Zealanders.

'The Picts and the Scots,' I said to myself, dredging items and images absorbed in early history lessons. The Angles. The Saxons. The Picts and the Scots. The Romans.

And the words of London fascinated me — the stacks of newspapers and magazines, sheets of advertisements in the windows of the tobacconists and newspaper shops, the names on the buses, the street signs, the illuminated advertising signs, the menus chalked on blackboards outside the humble Transport Cafés — Giant Toad and Two Veg., Shepherd's — the posters in the Underground stations and the graffiti in the public lavatories and road tunnels; the numerous bookshops and libraries. I had never had so much opportunity for public reading.

Nearer home, I enjoyed my Garden Room and the helpful company of Patrick. Each morning I crouched on the floor of the room waiting for the colour to surge into the electric plate to boil the kettle for washing and coffee, saving a shallow swill for rinsing the dishes, and then, following the example of a neighbouring tenant, I'd throw the dirty water into the gooseberry bushes that screened the rooms from the back lawn where the tenants from the main house hung their washing and on the rare fine afternoons sunned themselves in the company of the landlady's tortoise, it also trying to attract the smoke-filtered warmth of the now faraway sun.

The nights were cold. The stretcher bed placed low near the floor caught the night air that seeped with a taste of London fog between the cracks and beneath the ill-fitting door. I'd clear the resulting railway taste from my mouth and snuggle under the thin bedclothes with my warm coat spread on top. I was not too worried by the cold — I was in London, wasn't I? I had been to Crystal Palace, Ponders End, Piccadilly Circus, High Wycombe. I had walked on the Common and looked up at the city's second and third storey of trees and the September sun filled with blood. My destination of Ibiza now seemed years rather than weeks away. I had much to do: also I needed to find a job for a few weeks to earn more money. And so, listening to the distant roar of the traffic that I honestly thought was the sound of ocean waves breaking on an invisible shore, I planned my remaining time in London.

And as a cherished dream had been to visit Hampstead Heath and the neighbourhood where Keats had lived, one day I caught a bus to Hampstead Heath where I walked as far as the pond. The sky was grey, a mist hung over the city below, flocks of birds hurried through the sky in narrow formation as in a corridor, going somewhere towards the light; and the leaves trembled and tugged on the golden trees; and at the sight of the tall brown rushes growing at the edge of the pond I began to repeat to myself, naturally,

> O what can ail thee, knight-at-arms,
>   Alone and palely loitering?
> The sedge has wither'd from the lake,
>   And no birds sing.

I knew that I must have been one among thousands of visitors to London who had stood by the withered sedge, remembering Keats, experiencing the excited recognition of suddenly inhabiting a living poem, perhaps reciting it from memory, and then, as if rejecting a worn-out gift, with a sense almost of shame, banishing the feeling, then, later, going in search of it, reliving it without judging, yet always aware that too often everyone must tread the thousandth, millionth, seldom the first early layer of the world of imagination. Yet only the first day and night on earth could ever be thought of as the first layer on which the following secondary makers wove the shared carpet that in the peculiar arithmetic of making allows no limit of space for the known and unknown works of past and present and those, unfashioned, of the future. Looking down at London I could sense the accumulation of artistic weavings, and feel that there could be a time when the carpet became a web or shroud and other times a warm blanket or shawl: the prospect for burial by entrapment or warmth was close. How different it appeared to be in New Zealand where the place names and the landscape, the trees, the sea and the sky still echoed with their first voice while the earliest works of art uttered their response, in a primary dialogue with the Gods.

On Hampstead Heath I did not know whether to thank or curse John Keats and others for having planted their sedge, basil, woodbine and nodding violets, and arranged their perennial nightingales to sing in my mind. Misgivings (mis-givings) could not detract entirely from my first literary experience of London. That evening in my Garden Room I read and recited Keats and others (I having followed the advice of Jess Whitworth and joined the local Clapham Library and greedily accepted the rule — 'as many books as you wish').

Already, in practical pursuit of my literary aim I had bought copies of the *New Statesman*, the *Times Literary Supplement*, *John O'London's Weekly*, the *London Magazine*, the *Poetry Review*. (One wet day I visited the rooms of the Poetry Society where I gazed and gazed but did not enter.) I read exciting new poetry and prose by writers from the West Indies, some written in literary English, others with a West Indian version of English but all charged with a morning vision of London and the United Kingdom. I was much influenced by the West Indian writers and, feeling inadequate in my New Zealand-ness (for did I not come from a land then described as 'more English than England'?) I wrote a group of poems from the point of view of a West Indian new arrival and, repeating the experiment that Frank Sargeson and

I had made with the *London Magazine* when I pretended to be of Pacific Island origin, I sent the poems to the *London Magazine* with a covering letter explaining my recent arrival from the West Indies. The poems were returned with the comment that they were 'fresh, original' and the editor would like to see more of my work. The poems submitted did not quite come up to the standard of English required. I did realize that such literary pretences were a safeguard against the discovery by others that my 'real' poetry was worthless. They were also a reflection then of a New Zealander's search for identity beyond her own country where being thought 'more English than the English' was felt to be more insulting than praiseworthy. In a sense my literary lie was an escape from a national lie that left a colonial New Zealander overseas without any real identity.

Other practical matters, however, interrupted my poetic dreams. I had booked on the ferry to Dieppe, the train to Paris, a night in a Paris hotel, the train to Barcelona, the ferry across the Mediterranean to Ibiza — the journey was simple and done with if I said it quickly!

Next, I found work for two weeks as a housemaid/waitress at the Battersea Technical College Hostel where from six in the morning until noon my duties were to empty the ashes from the huge fireplaces, like brick altars, to clean and polish the ash-splattered floor, where, as it was now eight or nine in the morning, students walked to and from breakfast and lectures imprinting their footsteps in ash as if each trod unknowingly the slopes of Vesuvius, while I knelt, like a mountain-housemaid, scrubbing and polishing the world. When the students and staff had gone I cleaned the bedrooms that were often rich with incense as the hostel catered for Africans, from many countries, Indians, Egyptians, Arabs, each with a special religion, as well as for students from the British Isles. The household staff were mostly from London of English or West Indian origin. At the hostel I found myself unexpectedly living as if during the days of the Second World War.

When the meal known as 'lunch' (a substantial morning tea) was served at eleven o'clock each morning the household staff sat eating 'doorstep' bread and cheese sandwiches, drinking tea, and talking, first about the television programmes of the evening before, next about their experiences as Londoners during the Blitz. The discussion of the television programmes was clearly seen as an introduction to the major topic, and perhaps as a reassurance that the events to be so vividly recounted were now also in a shadow world of the past. Yet day after day the women talked of the war, reliving horrors they had never mentioned and could only now describe while I with a shuddering eerie sense of the overturning of time that one is often persuaded may flow so neatly from past to present to future, sat silently listening, feeling a growing respect for the relentlessness of experience that like a determined, pursuing, eternally embracing suitor will at last secure its match with speech, even if the process, as here, takes fifteen years' work in its refining, defusing, washing, drying of tears, change of content and view, preserving, discarding, undergoing death and rebirth. Perhaps if the war had not been a shared experience the memories might not have had the combined force that enabled them temporarily to abolish the present, nineteen fifty-six, the long wooden dining table, the students, the Technical College, and replace the group of household workers, mostly women between forty-five and fifty, with their former thirty-two-year-old selves, my contemporaries.

During those days I began to relive the war as the Londoners had known it. The relics were evident: bombed sites not yet rebuilt, overgrown with grass and weeds and scattered with rubble; the former Underground station with its hundreds of entombed Londoners caught in an air raid; squares and streets where death and destruction had now been given a place and names. My interest in the storytellers of Battersea made more tolerable for me the early morning waking in the now cold damp Garden Room, the walk through damp fog to the hostel, the thankless task of emptying the ashes, and in the evening, the waiting at the High Table, for tea during the week and high tea on Sundays. How old-fashioned the English are, I thought, as I stood by the 'low' tables waiting for a summons to attend to the High Table on its platform above the level of the rest of the room. The hierarchy was respected: no-one dared make a mistake in identifying rank or choosing the mode of address. I knew that in my past I'd witnessed similar behaviour in the mental hospitals where the doctors, matron and senior staff were regarded as gods; while I had looked thus on university lecturers and professors. At the hostel the fact that the surroundings were tailored to fit the superiority of some and the inferiority of others gave the system a permanence, locking everyone in place in a season of calm with not even the prospect of storm to dislodge and rearrange, while the argument against rearrangement lay always in the secure rewards of being already in place.

On days when I collected the mail from the Bank of New South

21

Wales in Berkeley Square, I exchanged opinions with other New Zealanders and Australians.

'What do you think of it all?' we'd ask.

The answer would be, 'The class system? They're in the Middle Ages.'

I felt, however, that the storytellers of Battersea were quietly arranging their own revolution, even without thought of past uprisings . . . the Picts and the Scots . . . the Angles . . . the Saxons . . . the Romans of Londinium . . .

Three

4

One afternoon when I was travelling on the now familiar 137 bus from Central London to Clapham Common (final destination Crystal Palace), I noticed a passenger staring at me, staring all the way to the Common, and when I left the bus he followed and fell into step beside me.

'I'm Nigel N.,' he said. 'I'm a law student. I live in Cedars Road.'

'I live in Cedars Road too,' I said primly but less primly than if he had been an apparent Englishman. I thought he looked old for a student, perhaps thirty-five, until I remembered that many of the students at the Technical College were men in their forties. Nigel was dressed in the manner of 'someone in the city' — dark striped suit, white shirt, white handkerchief, bowler hat, neatly furled umbrella used and flourished as a walking stick. There was a ludicrous striving about his appearance that roused my pity and made me ashamed for him.

'I'm from West Africa,' he said. 'Nigeria.'

'I'm from New Zealand.'

'Oh, New Zealand,' he exclaimed, beginning to list the facts of our landscape, bays, rivers, waterfalls; exports and imports; cities and their notable features. He was one of the few I had met in London who knew facts about New Zealand.

I listened admiringly to his recital and when he had finished, my silence told him the humiliating story of my ignorance of Africa and its peoples. Tarzan films. Painted warriors dancing about an intended human sacrifice intoning words that sounded like 'The Far Far Jungle, The Far Far Jungle . . . ' My adult life had little reference to life in Africa and thus I was forced to reach into childhood for myths and a curiosity that had been shut, like jewelled gates, from later education and daily experience and reopened only slightly by the works of Olive Schreiner, Doris Lessing, Dan Jacobson, Alan Paton, Nadine Gordimer, who despite their imagination and empathy were not writing from the unique point of view of native Africans.

And so when Nigel invited me to the cinema that weekend I accepted, a little nervously as I'd begun to feed on a range of London papers including *News of the World* and the *South London Press*, both lurid with detail of local domestic and street life. Nigel could be a pimp trying to lure me to Leicester Square, I thought. I'd already met the kerb-crawlers beckoning from their limousines, following persistently until I escaped into a less deserted street or a well-lit shop. I had a feeling of disquiet that I had allowed myself to be 'picked up' and I was thankful that I had chosen an afternoon session for our date at the cinema. I remembered how Nigel had stared at me, completely focussing his attention during the whole of the bus journey: perhaps in his culture this was a natural way of meeting people? I knew I was ignorant, colonial born and taught, yet passionately intent on learning about the rest of the world, 'them', the peoples who until now had been only statistics, stereotypes showered with equal concentrations of curiosity, fear, prejudice, mixed with the main brew of 'love your neighbour', 'we must love one another or die' — then why was I not looking forward to my Saturday afternoon at the cinema with Nigel?

We arranged to meet at the bus stop at Clapham Common where we took the 137 (coming from Crystal Palace) to near Leicester Square. Nigel was dressed smartly, again as a Londoner working 'in the city' and all he lacked to identify him as a city Englishman was the narrow leather briefcase initialled with gold, and the city-pale skin. I too wore the uniform of my group, the woman traveller who had listened to advice and read the brochures: I wore my jersey and skirt and coat and carried my Traveller's Joy handbag with its many compartments for travel documents, and no doubt, like Nigel, in time, once I felt safe in my new world I would discard my false uniform—already my handbag was more a burden than a joy with its heavy linings, brass buckles and clasps and extra straps for over the shoulder; why, it even had a lock and key.

I don't recall the name of the film except that it was a wide-screen epic popular then. We sat in the best seats, in the *Dress Circle*. The blue ceiling of the theatre, representing the sky, glittered with silver stars while music from an electric organ set on a platform beneath the stage played melodies from Rodgers and Hammerstein. During the interval (which I, rugby-bred, knew as 'half time'), Nigel, instead of rushing out to the foyer to smoke, bought ice creams, the best, with a swirl of chocolate on top, and as I sat licking my ice cream I looked around at the audience and as I noticed others doing the same, I felt a growing self-consciousness followed by a feeling of my own 'worth', a smugness because in 'going out' with someone from Africa I had shown myself free from racial prejudice. During my few weeks in London the newspapers and the radio referred constantly to 'racial prejudice' and so for the first time I was forced to consider my own feelings, and realizing the nature of my smugness I gave it sad recognition: I was no better than Patrick with his open bigotry. Why did it have to be?

The film ended. Nigel and I had sandwiches and coffee in a nearby 'Lyons' where again I felt self-consciousness, having read the London scandals about black women and white men and white women and black men, with the implication that the women were prostitutes, the black men, pimps, the white men unfortunate victims: the newspapers explained it all so neatly.

Trying to dissolve or dismiss my unpleasant feelings, I enjoyed Nigel's company. We shared much. We were both 'colonials' with similar education—heavy doses of British Empire, English history, products, rivers, cities, kings—and literature. He too had been given lists of the good, the strong, the brave, with friends and enemies clearly, permanently identified. He too had read of other places, other worlds with a mantle of invisibility cast upon his own world. I was more favoured, however, in having my ancestors placed most among the good, the strong, the brave, the friendly, in the position of the patronizing disposers, the blessed givers. We waited for the bus at Lower Regent Street.

'Let's sit upstairs,' Nigel said in a burst of eagerness.

I said primly (aware too of my tendency to motion sickness on the swaying upper deck of a London bus), 'No. I prefer downstairs.'

We sat downstairs, side by side on the long seat just inside the door — he, stiff-necked in his starched collar, I making casual conversation now and again, trying too hard to atone for my past unpleasant feelings. I sneaked a sideways glance at Nigel, just to look, a secret stare. His hands were lightly clenched, the sooty black rims closing upon a palm of black-smudged pink as if he had rose buds in each hand. Any feelings of 'duty', of necessary love, of sentimental contemplation of the abstract 'humanity' vanished when I saw this aspect of beauty. A cynic might remark, with Nigel wearing his English clothing, what more could bring him nearer to his apparent desire to be English, denying his origin, than a handful of rosebuds, the English flower? I wasn't cynical: I also was adopting English clothes, the word-clothes of Keats, 'Beauty is truth, truth beauty.'

We walked home beside the Common to Cedars Road.

'Come home and dance,' he said. 'We roll back the carpet and dance and dance.'

Feeling threatened, I said quickly, 'No thank you,' while a glance at his face told me that he thought of me as yet another racially prejudiced person.

'It's not that,' I said hurriedly. 'I've so much work to do. And thank you for the lovely afternoon.'

He smiled gently.

'You need to dance,' he said. 'You all need to dance and enjoy yourselves more. You English don't know how to enjoy yourselves.'

I didn't make the obvious reply, 'I'm not English, I'm from New Zealand,' for his observation was correct. I felt ashamed of my timidity. I knew I could have dined and danced and danced but I sensed also that the distractions of 'living' might threaten my desire and time to write. I was unwilling to take the chance.

Nigel and I parted coldly. I received a note from him saying he was sorry I had been unwilling to take the time to dance. I did not see him again. I remembered some lines of the verses returned from the *London Magazine*:

> *Now you light fires.*
> *The dancing woman wears amber beads*
> *and snip-snap the scissor cold*
> *shortens the hem of summer . . .*

and

He came from a far country
where they sit under lemon trees and ask
riddles of giant vermilion cattle with white faces . . .

The next week I accepted another invitation, again to the 'cinema', from Jack, an English physicist who lived in a basement room of the Main House and lectured at the Technical Institute. We went in the evening to a theatre in Clapham Junction where we sat in the back stalls. Again, I don't remember the name of the film. When the interval began, Jack, opening his mouth economically above small white teeth, said in a low voice, through his teeth, 'Would you like choc ice or plain.'

This ordinary question, 'Would you like choc ice or plain,' spoken with a London accent, seemed to be as full of revelation for me as had Nigel's recitation of English kings and queens and New Zealand mountains and rivers.

'And would you like a cornet?'

A cornet!

Cornet, high tea, indoors, pavement, Bear Right, Bear Left, Giant Toad and Two Veg. Do you travel by tube? Crystal Palace, High Wycombe, Tooting Bec, Wandsworth . . .

'She do look pretty, don't she?'

I was startled to find that Jack had lapses of grammar with usages that I'd been taught with such sternness were equivalent to criminal acts. I had not realized how deeply I had been persuaded that breaking the rules of language was a crime to be punished. I thought it unlikely that Londoners in all their races and cultures might live in fear of a split infinitive, a dangled participle, a misrelated clause all of which might bring upon them a *sentence*.

Jack and I ate our choc ices, oblong blocks covered with a brittle layer of chocolate and wrapped in silver paper, and sipped our orange drinks, then, when the film was over, we walked home to Cedars Road where, after drinking coffee in his room, I returned to my Garden Room. The next day, Saturday, when the sun came out and I was sitting by the gooseberry bushes, he came into the garden. He was formally dressed as many Londoners appeared to be, even at leisure, and he looked out of place lying in his city clothes on the rug I had spread on the lawn. He began to try to persuade the landlady's tortoise to come out of its shell, and as I watched the schoolboyish teasing and prodding of the tortoise I wondered could this tall pale man with his choc ices and cornets, his lapses in grammar, and now his pestering of the tortoise, really be a lecturer in physics? I had certain notions of how different professions must be and appear and my knowledge of people in the 'world' was still so meagre that I believed that such experts as physicists, doctors, lawyers were beyond displaying childish traits, and thus I found the behaviour of Jack, the physicist, almost incredible. I remembered the story of one of Tennyson's admirers who was shocked when Tennyson opened the conversation with a complaint about the price of coal.

Jack's behaviour depressed me by its ordinariness. I was shocked, too, by the way everyone at Cedars Road appeared to accept their dreary lives in gas-smelling rooms, their stained slop bucket and their 'good' water bucket, their seldom confessed loneliness that showed in the lingering way they clung to casual conversation as if words drifting by on stairs and in doorways must be snatched as a last hope. Although I was now one among them, I felt that I had a resource, an aim.

I also had the *Envoy*.

Had the tenants of the house in Cedars Road an Envoy, I wondered? I watched Jack, the physicist, as he jabbed at the tortoise.

'You'll hurt it,' I said.

He smiled, his lips opening slightly, like a door being opened yet alert for the intrusion of hostile air, debt-collectors, strangers.

'He doesn't feel it.'

The sun vanished then behind the gathering clouds. Evening came earlier each day. It was no use pretending that summer was not over. The leaves rattled harshly brittle in the trees. The gooseberries had long been gathered and the bushes were bare. I returned to my Garden Room to study the maps for my coming journey to Europe. The lengthening, darkening days, the damp chill of early morning and evening, the comforting presence of the many buildings in London, even the massed dreariness of the Cancer Hospital next door with its high wall backing on to the Garden Room, seemed to paralyse my desire to travel into the European winter. Perhaps, I thought, Spain, the South, would be different. I was deceived again by literature:

Oh for a beaker full of the warm South . . .

and

Swallow, swallow flying south . . .

My third encounter was with the artists of Parliament Hill Fields.

Letters from Frank Sargeson kept reminding me to visit the address given to us by the young couple who'd lived in Ibiza, and so one afternoon I telephoned Parliament Hill Fields and was invited to dinner that evening. I talked to Ben, a poet, who gave instructions about getting there, and again impatient with expectation aroused by names such as Parliament Hill Fields, Crouch End, I took the bus to a street of brick houses where Ben, a slim dark young man with thin hunched shoulders and long arms swinging to and fro like pendulums, guided me from the bus stop to the house.

His eyes were an intense brown, his face pale and moist.

'So you're from New Zealand?' he asked, looking at me as if to read the signs. He spoke with a Scottish accent.

'And are you Scottish?'

'Nay.'

'You sound Scottish.'

'Aye.'

He laughed then, explaining that he'd not long returned from his first visit to Scotland where he'd met *Hugh McDiarmid*.

'Hugh McDiarmid.'

'Oh?'

I knew that I should appear excited, perhaps amazed, admiring certainly but, sadly, I did not know of Hugh McDiarmid. I sensed that he was a poet. I remembered then a haunting poem in my *Golden Book of Modern English Poetry*, a reference to 'Stony Limits'. Hadn't that been written by McDiarmid?

'McDiarmid and James Joyce are my favourite poets,' Ben said in his soft Scottish accent, adding, 'Aye, Aye . . . '

'I am Polish,' he said as we walked to the front door of the house in Crouch End.

There were several tenants, male and female, all in London to further their artistic careers. They welcomed me, and after I had made my usual claim of being 'all the way from New Zealand', they asked me why I had come to London.

'I'm a writer,' I said with more certainty than I felt. 'I've a travel grant from the Literary Fund to further my experience.'

'Have you written any books?'

'Two,' I said, trying to sound casual.

'But have you had anything published?'

I realized that my new friends were not used to connecting writing with publication.

'You mean you've published a *book*?'

'A book of stories. And I've a novel being published soon.'

'Only in New Zealand,' I added hastily, trying to diminish their shock and restore plain curiosity to their faces. 'I'm hoping to get my novel published here some day.'

We were about to sit down to dinner. A young woman, an ample house-mother, put a huge bowl of fruit in the centre of the table. She returned with another of salad and one of cooked rice. She too stopped to stare when someone said, 'She's published a book!'

She called to the others in the kitchen as if summoning them to deal with an emergency. 'Quick. She's published a book!'

Those who were to share the meal came hurrying in. All stared at me. One explained, 'I've never met anyone who's published a book. I mean, someone like us.'

We began to eat.

'It's paella,' someone said. 'The Spanish dish.'

'Oh yes, I know,' I said eagerly. I was back in Sargeson country.

My new friends impressed me; they were gifted, intelligent, learned, more than I could ever hope to be, and, anxious to represent myself honestly in case there should be a misapprehension, I repeated that my book had been published 'only in New Zealand', while the novel would be available 'only in New Zealand'.

They asked the name of my publisher.

'Caxton for the first,' I said, 'and Pegasus for the novel.'

Their excitement about meeting a published author lessened as they admitted that already they had chosen their one and only publisher: Faber and Faber. Nothing less than Faber and Faber.

I confessed that I, too, dreamed of Faber and Faber.

'There's Deutsch, of course . . . and Michael Joseph . . . and Calder . . . ' Solemnly we raised our glasses of red wine in a toast to Faber and Faber, the supreme publishers of poetry.

They talked late into the night while I listened with wonder to their hopes and dreams of exhibition, performance, publication, for not all were poets; and when it was too late for me to catch a bus home to Cedars Road, they suggested I stay the night, sleeping in Mary's room. Mary had been Ben's girl, he told me, until he walked in one night to find her in the arms of Dora. He was sleeping alone now, Ben said, since he returned from Scotland and meeting Hugh McDiarmid. There was a flurry of midnight excitement as everyone focussed on Hugh McDiarmid. What a great poet, he was! The greatest, with Joyce, Yeats, T. S. Eliot . . .

'And Auden?'

'Oh, Auden! Yes.'

'And T. S. Eliot is the *head* of Faber and Faber!'

The excitement of the evening kept me awake when all had gone to bed, most with their chosen sleeping partners. Mary slept with her girlfriend, Dora, upstairs. I lay marvelling at the poetic dreams and the apparent confidence of those who seemed to become poets and painters simply by the spell of utterance: 'I'm a poet, I'm a painter.' I was impressed by the communal living, the freedom, the absence of demanding authority. I was surprised to find that some of the tenants were Londoners with their families living in London. Two of the girls were scholarship students at the Slade School of Art, while those without formal work while they pursued their chosen career, earned money (like Ben) as models in the art classes, and found much of their food by visiting the free sample areas of the Oxford Street and Knightsbridge stores where they munched crackers and caviar and tasted various pâtés and cheeses while no-one dared turn them away as they might have been eccentric millionaires in disguise.

Waking into the uninterested spurning light of day, I felt like a stranger in a household already preparing for the day's routine. Had I really toasted Faber and Faber among these self-possessed clever people whom in New Zealand I would never have dared approach unless I were safely in a corner at Frank Sargeson's while he took charge of the conversation?

I said a shy good morning. No, I wouldn't wait for breakfast. Then with promises to come again I said goodbye and hurried to the bus stop, losing my change purse on the way. Ashamed, panicking, I returned to the house.

'My purse, I dropped it. My money, my keys!'

I felt myself in a disarray that somehow might lessen my chances of ever being published by Faber and Faber or having my novel published in the United Kingdom, as if I had scattered words as carelessly as I scattered my purse, keys and money.

The artists of Crouch End had begun their day with that immuring process contracted by morning, already advanced, while I, exposed, felt unfixed and strange as I cried out again, like an intruder from a play, 'My purse! My keys! My money!'

Ben shook himself free to return with me to the bus stop and give me enough money for my fare.

Arriving at Cedars Road, unable to get through the locked gate, I rang the doorbell of the main house and Patrick Reilly came to my rescue by finding a spare key and, later, replacement keys.

'The Landlady need never know,' he said. 'Though it's not something I'd do every day.' Patrick was a man of judgment who referred all actions, including his own, to an unalterable set of rules, a first generation of rules with some of the second generation allowed occasional change or compromise. He was satisfied, I perceived, that my night away from the Garden Room had been innocently spent, although he frowned his disapproval when I said that my new friends were artists and poets.

'They're not the type for you,' he said. 'They hang around and do no work. And their morals are no better than they should be.'

'Oh no,' I protested, 'They *do* work.' And touched with their golden confidence I reminded him that I was a writer.

'You're different. When you come back from Spain to live in London, you'll be getting a *real* job.'

'Oh?'

'Yes. Peek Frean's are always looking for workers. Or you could be a shorthand typist.'

'Peek Frean's?'

'Peek Frean's.'

It seemed to me as if Patrick Reilly had sprouted from a handful of New Zealand earth that had found its way in my green haversack and spilled into the garden at Cedars Road. Patrick Reilly had helped me. He was now trying to take charge of me. He had accepted, against his will, that I was leaving for Ibiza, but he was firm in his plans for me to return 'fancy free' to London where I would find a decent job.

'We can look at our future then,' he said.

I said nothing. I did not really like Patrick Reilly. He reminded me of those I had lunched with in my far-off schooldays because there was no-one else available. Although he behaved with confidence and had firm opinions on almost every subject he impressed me as being yet another reject of a demanding world, although he might never have thought of himself this way. He knew he was a successful bus driver who had refused promotion to inspector because he did not care to stand at London bus stops freezing to death, flapping his arms to get warm while the buses passed with their drivers cosily sheltered from the weather. He preferred to be active, up there driving the bus, receiving messages from the conductor up top (one stamp with the foot, go, two stamps stop). All the same, he knew he was 'manager material'. He said so.

'There's no doubt that I'm manager material.'

He was clever, he spoke well, he could command attention, give orders. At home in his bedsitter with his best bluetop and Peek Frean's dark chocolate digestive biscuits and best Irish bacon and Irish butter, he retained his assurance and certainty.

Except, now and then, for a flicker of unease in his deep brown eyes, a wondering was it all so, as it seemed to be? Or was there perhaps something he had missed?

A
Game
of
Chess

5

During my last week in London I finished work at the Battersea Technical and said goodbye to the storytellers of Battersea. And on my last day in London, Ben, the poet, paid me a visit and after we had our tea and Peek Frean's dark chocolate digestive biscuits we began to talk about chess and discovered that we shared a delight in playing although neither of us had had a game for many weeks. I readily agreed when he said impulsively, 'Let's buy a set and play chess.'

We went in search of a chess set. The Clapham shops were closed, Clapham Junction was closed. We walked to Battersea, Chelsea, towards Sloane Square and still we could find no chess set for sale. Returning we tried Balham, Tooting, and the further we walked and the less likely our prospects became of finding a set, the more desperate our search grew. We both knew but did not say that the need for a game of chess had long ago delivered up its original impulse to become a symbol of those indefinable longings of one young man and one young woman, both aspiring poets, on an autumn afternoon in London. A game of chess would have anchored our longings, postponed our questions, for the time being ended our search. I remember clearly that strange afternoon. Ben with his long arms propelled in a kind of rowing motion was a quick walker and I hurried to keep up with him so that our pace was almost a run. An onlooker might have wondered, 'Why are that man and woman running through London on this autumn afternoon? What have they lost that they hope to find or who or what is pursuing them?'

We finally gave up. Still hurrying, we came to the flat where Ben's mother lived, a tiny upstairs flat in Hampstead. I felt disbelief and wonder that the small black-clad woman, the Polish emigrant who spoke no English, could be the articulate Ben's mother. Young men and women keep their parents so well hidden as if they stitched them in a sack inside their heart.

Upstairs in Ben's room we talked about books. He lay on the large double bed.

'My marriage bed,' he explained. 'When I find a Jewish girl to marry.'

He read from Hugh McDiarmid's poems and from *Ulysses*. And when I said it was time to leave, there was a feeling of regret, resignation, loss, as when we had failed to find our game of chess. He walked with me across the Heath to the bus stop and as we passed the pond I pointed to the withered sedge that was now one of my early memories of arriving in London, as if I had lived there now for many years. 'It was like this,' I said. 'And this.' Aware of the distortions of time that accompany departures.

My bus arrived. We said goodbye and promised to keep in touch. Our day had been a time of private intensity. We were acquaintances becoming friends. We sensed poetic movements within each other like two houses side by side where lights were turned on in different rooms and the occupants of each house, going their separate ways to different destinies, pause to recognize the neighbouring pattern of illumination.

I returned to the Garden Room to spend my last evening there. Patrick Reilly whom I'd not seen for several days was watching out for me.

'Let's go to the Common for a meal on your last evening,' he suggested.

'Well . . . '

We walked across the Common past the Outsize Dress Shop which Jess Whitworth, small in build, had patronized during her visits from

New Zealand, as brochures addressed to her were delivered regularly to the Garden Room. Latest news from the Outsize Shop.

We passed the huge secondhand bookshop, the ABC, the stationer's with the dusty fountain pens in a row in the window overlooked by the briefcases, the plastic toys, the dust-covered jigsaw puzzles. Finally we came to the restaurant that unlike the transport cafés where Patrick said he usually had meals, had tablecloths and a menu printed, not written on a blackboard outside.

I let Patrick choose. Steak medium rare with vegetables, followed by apple pie and cream.

The steak was large with shreds of thick fibre that displeased Patrick who complained, 'I expect it's horsemeat.'

I churned my mouthful and pulled a face.

'Surely not!'

'Oh yes, they often serve horsemeat if they can get away with it. I was hoping for a good Irish steak.'

I smiled to myself. Here was I, bred on the worship of the New Zealand butter god, and asking when I bought butter, 'Is it from New Zealand? I'm *all the way from New Zealand*,' while Patrick in his turn kept asking for Irish butter, bacon, steak.

Our conversation was dull. Patrick was homely and ordinary with little trace of romance or excitement, yet sometimes in the evenings when we had walked on the Common where the owners of the toy boats gathered to sail their craft by remote control, pressing buttons and switches as they stood in their macintoshes and sou'westers, although the evenings were mostly fine, Patrick had begun to talk dreamily of Ireland and the leprechauns. He'd seen them, he said, with his own eyes. I believed him, especially in the evening when the blood-red sun was dying, its edge balanced on the earth, and the leaves of the plane trees lay spread like withered hands relit, revived, on the paths and under the trees. When I became bored with Patrick or oppressed by his bigotry, I remembered the leprechauns and thought kindly of him.

The next day he took time from work to say goodbye at the station. 'Keep in touch,' he said. 'And stay fancy free.' His brown eyes were shining darker than usual, and I, softhearted, overcome by many goodbyes, felt tearful and sad to see him like another lost soul seemingly unaware of imprisonment or freedom.

The ferry where I had booked a sleeping berth steamed out into the Channel where it stopped halfway in a fog too dense to navigate.

The sea was calm. I heard the measured lapping of the waves and the foghorns calling one to the other like distressed seabirds.

At noon the next day, in slowly clearing fog, we anchored at Dieppe where I boarded the train to Paris.

Plaza
Roma

6

My first day in Paris is remembered for the tears I shed trying to make myself understood, and for realizing as I finally bought my bread, eggs, butter to cook on my small stove in the tiny attic room of the hotel overlooking the site of the old Bastille, that bread is indeed *pain*. I had been so well schooled in the mechanics of travel by Frank Sargeson remembering his walking tour of Europe and Jess Whitworth sharing her more recent overseas experience, that I obeyed their instructions exactly. The object, wherever I might be travelling, was to save money by cooking my own meals and, if possible, to stay in camping grounds or Youth Hostels, and so I had arrived in Paris with my pots and pans, a Girl Guide set of cutlery, tin-opener, pocket knife, cooking stove fuelled with sticks of methylated spirits, and sleeping bag with sleeping sheet. I'd also accumulated many books, secondhand and new, during my time in London, with a *Teach Yourself Spanish Part One* and a *Teach Yourself Spanish Phrase Book*. These, and my huge hooded fawn jersey, exercise books, a rug ('all travellers have a rug'), a supply of clothing, packed into my now bulging suitcases, with my typewriter in the green haversack, made my luggage a wearisome burden. I had chosen the hotel because it overlooked the Bastille and I wanted my two days in Paris to be spent not merely in organizing my travels and worrying over my pieces of luggage. I consoled myself by whispering loved passages of French prose and poetry and looking out of the tiny window at the wintry sky and reminding myself that I was in Paris. Who ever thought I'd be in Paris? I sang to myself part of the folk song 'Duncan Gray'.

> *You may go to France for me,*
> *Ha Ha the wooing o' it . . .*

And the next morning, refreshed and determined to purify in advance my memory of Paris I set out before dawn to explore the streets and after a time I found myself lost in the vegetable market of Les Halles, surrounded by cabbages, tripping over them, sliding on cabbage leaves, and unable to escape, for it was no use my reciting passages of Daudet, *Contes et Légendes*, Pierre Loti, Victor Hugo . . .

At last I found my way to the hotel where I prepared to take the night train to Barcelona.

At the station I stood in the queue at the counter marked *Consigne* where I hoped to *consign* my luggage to Barcelona, although I was surprised as I surrendered all but a small shopping bag and my Traveller's Joy that I was given a small numbered ticket without any inspection of my train ticket. Wasn't this unusual?

'Vous ne voulez pas regarder mon billet de travail?' I recited clearly, triumphantly.

'Non.'

Willing to accept that this must be the French way, I went to the platform, found my seat on the train, and waited, looking out now and then, as anxious travellers do, to try to identify my luggage among the trolleys being wheeled to the goods van.

On the long seat opposite me were an elderly man and a small boy, very frail, who lay covered with a blanket, his head in the old man's lap. The boy had been in Paris for an operation on his heart, the man said. Now and again throughout the journey he selected grapes from a bag and fed them one by one to the boy who opened his mouth for them, like a young bird.

'These are good for him,' the old man said. 'They will make him well.'

The other passengers in the compartment, two middle aged Spanish women travelling to Perpignan, talked in Spanish to each other for several hours, then fell asleep, while I drowsed now and again. The old man stayed awake, vigilant, upright, occasionally adjusting the blanket over the boy, so that even when I drowsed I'd open my eyes to see the old man's alert pale face and his intent dark eyes. The women glanced often at the two and made sympathetic murmurings about the sleeping boy.

Morning came, and we approached the Spanish border, and I was content to abandon my own description of my journey in remembering the acute observation of Maurice Duggan's *Diary of a Journey*. For me, this was Duggan country. I remembered Duggan's description of train, guards, sea, sky, earth. The landscape was his, and these were his border guards (with occasional contributions by Lorca and Lawrence Durrell) moving with flashing guns, polished buckles and boots, ushering the passengers into the customs hall where the experience again became uniquely my own.

I inspected and re-inspected the unclaimed suitcases. No familiar green haversack, no two old suitcases with their straps of New Zealand leather.

'Mes bagages,' I said wildly to no-one in particular. 'Je les ai consignés de Paris.'

I approached an official.

'Mes bagages?' I said.

The official shrugged.

'Consignés,' I said.

After a halting exchange of phrases I realized that I had deposited my luggage in the left luggage department at the Paris Station and the ticket I held was my ticket of deposit.

A sweeping cloud of tears threatened but did not fall. I gulped. Then, in spite of growing apprehension and a feeling of lonely misery, I was overtaken by the delight of being free of luggage. I watched the other passengers struggling to climb into the high Spanish train and my sense of freedom increased. Lighthearted now, I could have flown on my own wings to Barcelona and Ibiza.

Frank Sargeson had written to his friend, the writer Greville Texidor, who lived in Spain, telling her of my visit. I was met at Barcelona by Greville's daughter, Christina, who with her husband, the painter Paterson, took me to lunch at La Plaza Roma, remembered as an old square lined with grey eucalyptus—or were they olive?— trees with the surrounding buildings standing like ancient earthforms, earth-coloured, with their roots deep in the red soil. There appeared to be a dust of sun fallen over everything, with the square enclosed in quiet, like a private pathway to other times. Unburdened by ridiculously beleaguering luggage, I felt my being untethered, my senses sharpened by my night of waking. I was aware not of the noise and traffic of Barcelona but of this background of overflowing quiet that enveloped me with a feeling of being at home, in place at last, like a piece of human furniture that has been shifted and reshifted and rearranged, never before exactly right, in all corners of the world. I did not know yet whether this was the common experience of travellers, in response to foreignness, difference, an abrupt removal of all tethering and bonds to a native land.

Later I met Greville and her husband and their twelve-year-old daughter at their city apartment where I sat smiling, empty-headed and shy. I met also Colin, introduced as an English poet, who was returning to Ibiza on the same boat and who had kindly offered to make sure I found somewhere to stay.

'A room for a few nights,' he said. 'Una *habitacion*.'

'Una habitacion,' I repeated nervously, aware that I knew nothing of Spanish.

That evening I saw Colin, briefly, as I boarded the ferry. The boat seemed frail, a cockleshell, the Spanish night was dark, *obscure*, the sea was dark, calm with small clumps of waves rocking and glinting white like a rooted bed of flowers, asters or Queen Anne's lace. I hurried to my sleeping berth and waited, sleeping most of the night until morning.

Calle
Ignacio
Riquer

7

When I woke the ferry had already entered the harbour of Ibiza and was preparing to anchor. Colin was there waiting for the gangplank to be put in place. Some passengers had already leapt ashore without waiting.

And twenty minutes later there was Colin revving his scooter and calling to me, 'Climb on the back. I'll take you to a small hotel I know.'

Boldly I climbed on the back saddle and clinging fast to Colin's waist and with some alarm as I'd never ridden a scooter, I swayed back and forth as we roared up and down the narrow cobbled streets stopping in front of a small pension.

'Here,' he said. 'You can stay here for a few nights, there's sure to be a vacant room.'

He led me to the reception desk where he spoke fluently in Spanish, received a reply, and turned to me.

'Two nights?'

'That's fine,' I said.

Then, his duty discharged he returned to his scooter, restarted the engine and roared away up the street while I, feeling lost with my vanity hurt, watched him go. He might at least have said he would see me again or it was nice to meet me or good luck with my writing. Well, he knew Spanish and they'd said, with respect, that he was a *poet*. And who was I? Only a friend of a friend of a friend.

I stood in my room smelling the pervasive Ibicencan smell that I could not yet identify, feeling tired, anxious about finding a *permanent* place to stay, inferior because I was not a poet, but, overturning all these feelings, was my eagerness to begin my new life in a foreign land.

First, I needed a phrase book that was not directed entirely at the rich buying, skiing, photographing, share-accumulating traveller likely to be a paratrooper going bankrupt, being measured for a new suit, who is struck by a thunderbolt while suffering from a fractured skull at the railway station.

And so, joyously, because I had no luggage to take care of, I went in search of a bookshop where I bought a tissue-paper-thin edition of the *Daily Telegraph*, several Spanish newspapers, Paris newspapers, and a phrase book of Catalan, *Learn Spanish With Me*, which I then used to buy bread, butter, cheese, an apple and a banana. I bought also a cake of chocolate costing more than the sum of the other foods. It had creatures inside it, waving their tiny heads from their tiny nests.

When night came I discovered that the one small ceiling light in my room was so dim that I could barely see the outline of the furniture, and when I looked into the street below, I saw that the shops were candle-lit, with all lights dim. I slept then, and woke full of anticipation for my first 'pure' morning in Ibiza. I would walk, I decided, in search of a place to stay.

I walked towards the old city on the hill, along the narrow cobbled streets to the remains of the Roman wall with its stone figure of a Roman warrior at the entrance to the tunnel leading to the upper city. Walking carefully to avoid the piles of dog and human mess in every corner, I came into the daylight of the hill where I looked down on the harbour and the buildings across the harbour, perfectly mirrored in the clear tideless ocean. At the top of the hill I could see the other side of the island beyond the fields and olive groves to the transparent Mediterranean. I sat leaning against a grey rock that was massed like an accumulation of layers of ancient olive leaves. I shared the solitude with a small herd of wild goats, and the silence with the distant sound of the fishing boats. The grey-leaved olive trees with their twisted branches and trunks turned in defence against the sea wind, and the white-grey stones like long-fallen snow that had refused to melt, on the red soil beneath the trees, drew from me a feeling of tenderness as if this land were mine and I had known it long ago. It was, of course, Shelley's world, and I had known it in poetry, and they were Shelley's phrases that came first to mind allowing me the—parasitic—indulgence of reunion with 'Ode To the West Wind',

> Thou who didst waken from his summer dreams
> The blue Mediterranean, where he lay,
> Lulled by the coil of his crystalline streams,
> Beside a pumice isle in Baiae's bay,
> And saw in sleep dim palaces and towers
> Quivering within the wave's intenser day . . .

before clearing the space where I wanted my 'own' thoughts to be. It was tempting, however, to sit remembering my first ice-clean exposure to poetry, like the first spring of all time, and for the moment I was happy just to *be* where I had always felt most at home—outside, under the sky, on a hilltop overlooking the ocean; and I might have sat there, as I used to sit for hours had I not remembered the purpose of my walk—to find a place to stay.

I followed the narrow path along the bowed ridge of the hill where the storms had struck more harshly and the bowed vegetation showed its agonized struggle to grow in the face of the wind with little roothold except in the crevices in the snow-grey rock.

As I walked I saw two figures in black shawls, stockings and shoes, bending to gather twigs and branches to heap into their large woven baskets, and again I recognized them because I had known them before—in paintings depicting the toil of peasants or as casual onlookers in the midst of a miracle, or in descriptions by Victor Hugo and Pierre Loti and Daudet. The two women furnished the landscape as if it were an interior long ago formed, decorated, occupied with no prospect of change.

Consulting my new phrase book, I murmured, 'Buenos dias.'

'Buenas tardes,' one replied, pointing to the sun.

I spoke hesitatingly, 'Jo soy de Nueva Zelanda. Janet. Quiero habitacion.' I placed the palms of my hands together and rested them against my cheek.

The two women began to talk excitedly together. They turned to me. 'El Patron,' they said. 'El Patron.'

I gradually understood that they were *Catalina* and *Francesca* and I was *Janetta*, and they would take me to their *patron* who would rent his house to me. I dissolved any suspicions they might have had when I explained that I was not a *tourist* — 'No soy turista,' I said firmly. 'Soy *escritora*.'

Grasping me lightly by the arm, Catalina led me down the hillside through the narrow cobbled streets to *Ignacio Riquer* where, they said, the house was next to theirs. El Patron was in charge of the Museum and his brother *Fermin* was in charge of the house where I might be able to stay. At Number Six Ignacio Riquer they pushed open a heavy unlocked front door. A starved-looking cat sitting on the wooden table in the kitchen lashed at us with its claws as it vanished in a streak of grey.

'Los gatos,' Francesca said angrily, explaining that they were wild cats who would attack me if I left the door open. Would I wait, Catalina asked, while they fetched El Patron?

Within five minutes they had returned with El Patron's brother, Fermin, slightly built and in his mid-forties, who appeared to be agreeable to my staying in the house and who named a rent comparable to that mentioned by Frank's friends in New Zealand who had stayed on Ibiza, and after Fermin had shown me the room where I could sleep, and the lavatory at the end of the terrace, and the kitchen (there was no bathroom), I said I'd return to my hotel to pick up my shopping bag. I understood that I was renting the entire house. Later when I arrived with my shopping bag and my Traveller's Joy, Fermin was in the sitting room overlooking the terrace, playing a violin. He stopped playing as I entered. He looked surprised by my lack of luggage. I hastily turned the pages of my phrase book.

'No hay equipages,' I said. 'A Paris.'

At last I was able to explain that my luggage had been deposited at the Paris railway station and I'd be sending for it and if all was well it should arrive within two weeks. I explained that I was an *escritora* and my typewriter was in my luggage. I came from New Zealand, Nueva Zelanda, I said, the land of sheep, wool, butter . . . I tried to give the impression that New Zealanders were unlike the rest of the world in being clean, pure, unprejudiced, well disposed towards all members of the human race. And New Zealand was a beautiful country. It was *God's Own Country*.

Fermin understood. He frowned. Ibiza, he said, was also *God's Own Country*.

I knew that in speaking thus of New Zealand I was showing little sense or perception, but to affirm New Zealand in this way was habitual to one who had been taught so insistently to equate survival with sheep, wool, butter, or, rather, death with the failure to export sheep, wool, butter: *export or die*.

Fermin was sympathetic about my luggage. He undertook to make it his duty to inquire each morning at the waterfront for news of it. He came to the house each day, he said, to practise the violin as he played it each evening in a nightclub. Other members of the household also came to the house, he said, while the servants Catalina and Francesca who lived next door would use the kitchen for their cooking, as usual.

At least, I thought, in spite of the comings and goings, I'm the only occupant.

My bedroom was large and airy with a wide window overlooking the harbour and the distant shore where the buildings lay like those of another city, a sea or mirror city reflected in the clear water. I arranged a table and chair for writing and I thought with some excitement of the new book I'd begun in Auckland, *Uncle Pylades*, and the one I planned to write following that. My first task, however, was to write to American Express in Paris enclosing my left luggage ticket with instructions to them to collect and forward my luggage. Next, I needed a change of clothing.

I wrote and mailed my letter to Paris, then I shopped for underwear, stockings, a skirt, jersey, nightgown and writing materials and when I arrived home, laden with parcels but bewildered that the shops would no longer accept my money, Fermin, inspecting the limp pile of pesetas, explained that someone had given me 'old' money, pre-1935, that was no longer legal tender.

'It's worth nothing,' he said. 'You've been tricked.'

I sat again at my desk. I wrote poems and some letters, the kind of inspired letters travellers send from a new country where everything glistens with marvel. For me, that marvel was the light, the sky, the colour of the olive trees and of the buildings thumbed and worn like old stone pages, with none of the restlessness of New Zealand buildings, none of the sensed fear of sudden extinction by earthquake or volcano. These rose like opened books on a lectern of earth and were turned perhaps once in a hundred years, their certainty lying in their age and their openness. And crowning the marvel was the receptiveness of the tideless ocean admitting to its depths the entire world standing on its shores, creating a mirror city that I looked upon each day.

Without my typewriter I felt limbless, and it was good news when I heard that my luggage was on its way to Ibiza. I happened that day to be walking past a café when I saw Colin, the English poet, sitting with friends at one of the tables on the footpath, and I did not realize until I saw him how miserably lonely I'd been feeling without my typewriter and my luggage and with my several hundred worthless pesetas. Mildly self-conscious but trying to hide it, I strolled past his table and looked towards him. 'Oh,' I said, in a tone of surprise. 'Hello again.' Then in a burst of excitement, I said rather more loudly than I had meant to, 'My luggage is coming soon! And I've found a place to stay!'

His friends stopped in their eating and drinking to stare. At first Colin did not seem to recognize me. Then he said coolly, dismissively, 'Oh, hello.'

He simply stared, showing no delighted response at my news.

I may have exaggerated his coolness; I certainly remember it. I felt a chill current swirling about me and I wished I had said nothing. He and his friends were so much in place there, drinking at the kerbside café table, just as Maurice Duggan, sophisticated and clever, had described, and as Frank Sargeson had recalled to me, saying, 'It's the continental way.'

I hurried away from Colin, the English poet, and his friends, and after my rebuff I made no attempt to mix with or meet the English-speaking colony. I therefore spoke only in Spanish and French, coached by Catalina, originally from Algeria, who also spoke French, and by Francesco, Fermin, and José, the twenty-year-old son of El Patron, a law student, who came each week to the house to bath in the tin tub in the kitchen and who, after his bath, came to my room to try to teach me Spanish.

Each morning when Fermin finished practising his violin he also taught me a few words and phrases of Spanish, and sometimes he reminisced about his past. He unlocked one day a large cupboard, drawing out the double doors to reveal a lit interior with carvings of the crucified Christ, on shelves, and pinned to the inside of the door, a poster of a young handsome General Franco, El Caudillo.

'He saved us from the Communists,' Fermin said. 'He was younger then. And I was young.'

47

He shrugged and looked ashamed.

'Things are different now. It was long ago. Mirra.'

He led me to the window that like my bedroom window overlooked the city and the sea and, nearer, the road leading from the Roman tunnel to the church on the hill. He pointed to the stone wall bordering the road.

'The Stations of the Cross,' he said. 'El Caudillo lined up all the Communists there and shot them. I saw it. But I was a young man. It's different now. And El Caudillo . . . '

Fermin shrugged and went to the cupboard. I thought he was about to spit on the poster. Instead, he ripped El Caudillo from the wall and thrust the crumpled poster on the lowest shelf of the cupboard. Then he shut the door and locked it.

'Those are my carvings in there,' he said. 'I'm an artist too. But it's different now.'

As each day passed and I occupied myself with writing poems and letters and stories, telling myself that when my luggage arrived with my typewriter I'd begin work on my book, Fermin would bring news of my luggage, for each morning he inquired at the wharf. My luggage and his secret cupboard locking away the dreams of a younger man became our bond. And one day he came to me with a small box closely packed with small religious pictures.

'This is another treasure,' he said. 'Which Saint would you like, Janetta?'

I hesitated.

'Oh. St Francis.'

He found the picture of St Francis and gave it to me.

'These are long ago too,' he said . . .

So what have I seen in memory? Memory is not history. The passing of time does not flow like a ribbon held in the hand while the dancer remains momentarily still. Memory becomes scenes only until the past is not even yesterday, it is a series of retained moments released at random. I am remembering Fermin's face as he spoke of his once-passionate hate of the Communists, how in showing me the Stations of the Cross where the executions had taken place, he talked not of distant enemies with a vaguely fearful ideology but of friends and neighbours, even relatives, and how he had approved the killing because the orders came from his beloved Caudillo. Now he was shocked, saddened, and unsure whether the killing had been necessary.

He could not even tell of his doubts through the medium of his violin. He may have known that his family laughed at his violin playing, or smiled tolerantly when they happened to hear him. I smiled politely, murmuring a phrase that might have been 'Bueno, Bueno.'

I still see Fermin's troubled face as he stares from the window at the Stations of the Cross.

Soap-
New
People

8

The time of waiting for my luggage and typewriter became my apprenticeship to the life of Ibiza and the family of El Patron.

With a gesture of poetic greed I bought a book entitled *Las Mil Mejores Poesias de La Lengua Castellana (1154-1954)* which I showed to José, asking, 'Where are the poets of Ibiza? Has Ibiza any poets?'

The island of Formentor, covered with pine trees and lying just south of Ibiza, had a poet, José said. Miguel Costa Llobera. I therefore found the one poem by Llobera, 'El Pino de Formentor', which José read aloud and I later learned by heart. It became my 'set piece', my focus, even more than the poems of Lorca included in the anthology, for an Ibiza that I found to be so old, touched by the Moors and the Romans, and as young as childhood's blue-sky days.

> *Hay en mi tierra un arbol que el corazon venera;*
> *de cedro es su ramaje, de cesped su verdor,*
> *anida entre sus hojas perenne primavera . . .*

and

No asoma por sus ramos la flor enamorada,
no va la fuenticilla sus plantas a besar;
mas banase en aromas su frente consagrada
y tiene por terreno la costa acantilada,
por fuente el hondo mar.

Laboriously I searched my new dictionary for definitions before I wrote my poetic translation of 'El Pino'. Llobera was a 'safe' poet, a patriot, not a rebel. Fermin and José approved of my choice of a poet who wrote of pine trees, and I wondered if I had not, in part, come home to my own childhood when I remembered other times I had never known by writing, twenty years earlier.

A memory, a forgotten day
so full of spring sunshines.
Told by trees that gently sway
and whispered by the pines.

The traveller to new lands has a rare opportunity to revisit or visit other times, for

soap-new people come and go
washing away the stale time's flow
in an heap to eternity . . .

José's mother and sister rarely came to the house: their lives were sheltered. Although I was a single woman, alone, I was still a foreigner, and everyone knew that the ways of women from foreign lands were not those of Spanish women. I was approved of, however, because I was not a tourist, I was not American, I was an industrious *escritora* who did not have foreign friends, while there was a homelessness about me because my luggage and my typewriter had gone astray: my misfortune had become my advantage. Catalina and Francesca therefore took charge of me, and each morning when the fishing boats came in with their catch, Catalina and Francesca taught me how to choose the best fish, what to ask for, how much to pay. The tiny silvery fish, like sardines, cost one peseta for five. Later, the two women showed me how to cook the Ibicencan dishes, and I was now able to think back in astonishment and some embarrassment at my early purchases of butter and chocolate. Early in my stay, arriving home with butter, I met Francesca cooking her tea and I was dismayed and saddened by the way she stared at the butter in my basket.

'Mantequilla!' she said in awe.

Only the rich bought *mantequilla*.

I had also bought a strip of steak.

'*Carne*. Oh Janetta!'

I shared my butter and meat and when Catalina came for her tea I heard them talking excitedly about *Janetta* who had bought *mantequilla* and *carne*!

As I learned to live on the Ibicencan diet there was no longer cause for amazement and curiosity about my food. I copied Francesca and Catalina, also, in the fuel I bought for the fire. Whereas in New Zealand, I thought of coal and wood arriving in sacks on laden lorries, here I took my woven basket with the long handles to queue with the blackgarbed and shawled women for a small basket of coke and perhaps two or three small blocks of wood. Yet Francesca's eyes still glittered as she watched me arrive home with my full basket, as if I had a natural permanent abundance granted me. Even when my supply was low, her glance made me ashamed, reminding me of the hungry stare of the alley cats that still waited outside the door for a chance to get in, and each morning followed the rubbish collector as he led his donkey, the paniers overflowing, up the narrow street to the hilltop and the other side of the island.

This was my first encounter with the feelings of the really poor, and with my own awareness that I had the means to travel, I could support myself for several months, I could return to New Zealand to the world of plentiful electricity where people lived in houses surrounded by gardens of fruit, vegetables and flowers; and that in spite of my constant refrain, *No hay mucho dinero*, I belonged to a rich nation. I may not have been a rich *turista* spending money on hotels, wining, dining, clothes, but my homeland was then rich in opportunity, in compassionate legislation that took account of everyone's need for food, shelter and for wealth as distinct from ill-health. Before I left New Zealand, Frank Sargeson had said, 'There'll be the poor, and the beggars. If you start thinking about them you'll go mad. You have to try to forget them. There's nothing you can do.'

What could I have done to improve the lot of Francesca and Catalina? Butter and meat every day? I could not bear the way they searched my clothes with their eyes as if I might be wearing concealed jewels. Francesca's dark eyes, in particular, had an alertness I'd not seen before in a human being—she was the hungry one eager for goods as well as food she could not buy. And yet there was seldom a sign of discontent unless it was revealed one day when, riding my hired bicycle along the dusty white country roads by the olive groves, I met Catalina and Francesca who must have walked many miles, gathering the olives that had fallen from overhanging branches into the road. There were others too, families from the city who had come with their baskets to pick up the olives. Catalina and Francesca explained that this was their chance to supply themselves, and when Catalina said wistfully that El Patron had a farm in the country and I asked if the family gave her vegetables, eggs, fruit, she said, 'Oh no, we buy them from the market. The farm is for El Patron and his family; but we are always allowed to collect the olives that fall in the road.' I glanced into their basket at the small, hard, pitted fruit, and I constructed for myself a proverb that, in the way of proverbs, would try to solve everything: the olives that fall to the side of the dusty road are the tastiest, the most treasured. Words again came to the rescue.

Imagining that the Balearic Islands, the *Spanish Islands*, were by definition always blessed with sun, perpetual summer, I had given little thought to winter clothing, and as the days, still blue and sunny, became colder I was glad to have my outsize fawn jacket with its big pockets and hood, and once I had explained to Catalina and Francesca that wearing slacks did not make me a female devil (*diablas* was their word for the foreign women in their black slacks), I began to wear the grey slacks I'd been given in New Zealand, and the warm brown coat bought by Aunties Joy and Elsie.

It was near Christmas when my luggage arrived by sea. When Fermin brought the news there was great excitement and when the truck delivered the two suitcases and the green canvas haversack, and Fermin carried everything through to the sitting room, Catalina and Francesca and José, fresh from his bath, came to stare, expecting me to open the cases at once. Confronted with goods that, except for my typewriter, I had now convinced myself were no longer necessary I felt embarrassed as if I were meeting friends I no longer wished to know because we had outgrown the friendship. I felt I should compensate the family for their obvious disappointment: three months of waiting and wondering and asking, and now these old battered cases, crushed at the corners, one lid askew, as if, like some objects in old fairytales, they had manoeuvred themselves miles along roads and across seas to reach Ibiza.

When later in the privacy of my room I opened the suitcases, I looked distastefully at everything I had packed. Then, as I saw again my books, the small stove, the Girl Guide cutlery, the army pots and pans, I felt more kindly towards my outcast luggage. Ah, there was the blue 'tube' dress I had sewn from a length of jersey silk, the material that 'everyone' in New Zealand was wearing. Now the colour appeared too bright and out of place in a land where clothes were black.

And because I could not deny Catalina and Francesca the chance to see the 'goods', I invited them in. I showed them my typewriter. And here was the green velvet dress that my sister had made from a curtain.

Catalina and Francesca laughed.

'Janetta's cortina, Janetta's cortina.'

I retrieved my rug and hot-water bottle to make good use of both for apart from the kitchen fire there was no heating in the house and the vast marble floors were now permanently chilled, and the nights were very cold. And now that I had my typewriter, I felt that I could *really* begin work instead of writing poems and letters and stories. I was aware, however, that I had invested more in the arrival of my luggage than it could ever accommodate, that I had been practising the oldest form of self-deception, appeasing the present by clinging to an event in the future: I was in good human company.

The
Pine
Trees

9

In the days that followed I sat wrapped in my rug, nursing my filled hot-water bottle while I typed my novel, *Uncle Pylades*. I looked out of the window at the children playing hopscotch under the eucalyptus trees, the markings for the game drawn with a stick in the white dust. I listened to the chanting

> *Tengo tengo tengo*
> *tu ne tiene nada*
> *tengo mantequilla* . . .

and I watched the elder sisters sitting in the doorways, their lace pillows propped on their knee, working their lace bobbins, hands swiftly passing one bobbin over the other, and I thought of that time in hospital when I had made French lace, gathering from the French instructions a feeling that although I was being denied books and writing and ordinary human conversation, new life was being channelled to me through those instructions in the *Manual of Lacemaking: Plantez un épingle au point Deux . . . jetez trois fois . . .*

Language that had betrayed, changed, influenced, could still befriend the isolated, could help when human beings had withdrawn their help.

Thunderstorms came crashing above the house, lightning played vividly in the room, and winds wailed, cried, screamed as I'd never heard winds, reminding me of the ancient gods, creatures born of thunder, lightning, storm, raging up and down the windowpanes as if trying to get in, clawing the glass, mouthing it as if it were an instrument of music. Often, in the midst of the storm, I'd walk outside, up the street to the other side of the island and I'd sit on the grey rock among the battered silver-grey plants and trees, and I'd think that I had never felt so much at home. I rejoiced that I was alone on a Mediterranean island, speaking no English, with my Spanish welcomed as my English had never been, for my struggle to express my thoughts was attended by the kindness of those who were proud that I was trying to speak their language and who were eager to explain, suggest, help, and teach, whereas in speaking one's native language to others who also speak it one is alone, struggling to meet the expectations of the listener.

As I sat at my table typing, I looked each day at the city mirrored in the sea, and one day I walked around the harbour road to the opposite shore where the *real* city lay that I knew only as the city in the sea, but I felt as if I were trying to walk behind a mirror, and I knew that whatever the outward phenomenon of light, city, and sea, the real mirror city lay within as the city of the imagination.

I thought much about islands and seas. I wrote a verse,

> *Pity the banished continent estranged from sea*
> *where people longing for mirror capture*
> *behind their eyes a mountain plain or valley*
> *that shifts with the tides of seeing*
> *in snowshapes and masses of cloud, never wholly*
> *growing apart from the shadowy ponderous*
> *land stooping, itself in shadow, to drink the day's light.*
>
> *Small are islands, forever fluid in image*
> *known best once only, over the shoulder*
> *as birds flying or rabbits crouched, thumping the sea;*
> *each day a stranger shape within the mirror,*
> *more completely shining and misting over*
> *than broken shadows from centuries, than moveless wings*

of a giant bird or the one whole leaf discarded
from a tree whose whole form and seeking
of invisible sky are held flickering
beyond the communion of water
even on a calm day of a quiet inland sea.

Small are islands, a tyranny of completeness,
a fear of meeting too many selves in mirrors.

Oh how seriously I took my dream of being a poet! I'm on my own now, I told myself. I'm living the life of a writer. I felt at peace within my own mind, as if I were on an unearthly shore, seeing the creation of scenes from the great paintings of the world, the people of Ibiza moving as if directed by the painters, with the houses, the plants, the day and night skies each the colours the painters would have chosen. In my afternoon walks or cycling I marvelled at the way the clear perimeter of the island unfolded before my eyes. I wrote ecstatic letters to Frank Sargeson. Ibiza, I said, was all they claimed it would be and all I dreamed. I felt it contained within me and when I had explored the beaches and the salt mountains I cycled past the fields of clay where the clay surface opened its red vein, at the pottery works, and leaving my bicycle, I walked to the wooded interior of the island, to a mass of light-green pine forest where, Catalina and Francesca warned me, the bandits and wild men roamed, and although I did not believe them, I discovered later that they spoke the truth—Ibiza, like Sicily, had its bandits.

Sometimes during my walks in town I saw and heard the foreigners laughing, talking, and I wanted to cry out to them, 'I'm here, I also speak English. I'm from New Zealand, *all the way from New Zealand.*' Instead, I passed haughtily by as if I knew everything in the world.

I could not believe the gentleness of Ibiza. In the evening when the supply of electricity was reduced and the shops were candle-lit, I'd walk without fear around the dark streets of the city. When I had asked for a key to the front door, Fermin, Catalina and Francesca had stared in surprise, explaining that only foreigners locked their doors, the secretive, possessive foreigners guarding their wealth, their large supply of *dinero*. My front door, therefore, was always unlocked.

Christmas came with a letter and a food parcel from Patrick Reilly in London. He sent corned beef and Irish stew and he hoped I was still fancy free.

With Christmas also, the sound ceased that had persisted for many days, a cry like a small sharp succession of cheers, a chorus of 'Bravo, Bravo, Bravo,' which had puzzled me and which I thought were the cries of the island dogs that like flesh-coloured almost transparent shadows ran at intervals through the streets. I learned that the cries had been those of the turkeys in the small yard beneath the house where now there was silence. I wrote:

> *Christmas and Death are hungry times*
> *when only the foolish and the dying*
> *with circumscribed vision of Here*
> *learn complete praise, saying*
> *Bravo Bravo to the Invisible.*
>
> *Who knows to what in the small yard*
> *the turkey gives violent praise?*
> *Or the sick man spread*
> *on a white plate in his diminishing world?*

And with the bitter cold came a new sound, the almost ceaseless tolling of the church bells and I'd look out to where the small white coffins were carried in the many funeral processions. Each day as the tolling began, Catalina or Francesca would sigh, murmuring, 'Ah, un crio, un crio.'

Many *crios* died that winter: it seemed to be usual. The cypress-bordered cemetery on the road to the interior was lined with new graves.

And so I wrote, and I walked — in the evening to the hilltop where I watched the small dark shapes of the bats swinging to and fro like threads out of the sky.

And once, cycling, I stopped to rest at a small pine-bordered beach where I lay under the trees and listened to their hush-hush, and the light fell like blue and green snow around and upon me, and the sea glittered through the pine branches. Not an unusual scene but, as in my visit to the pine forests of the interior, it touched the antenna reaching from childhood, just as childhood contains its own antennae originating in conception and the life of the dead and the newly begun; and feeling the sensation at the nerve ending and its origin in the past among the pine trees and sky and water and light, I made this scene a replacement, a telescoping with the trained economy of memory, so that from then and in the future the memory of this scene contains the collective feeling of those past, and now when I listen to pine trees by water, in light and blue, I feel the link, the fullness of being and loving and losing and wondering, the spinning 'Why was the world?' that haunted me in childhood, the shiver of yesterday, yet I remember the pine trees of Ibiza.

Christmas that tends to block the view ahead having passed, I began to think with a nagging anxiety of my 'future'. When my grant had been used, I supposed that the accepted move would be a return to New Zealand, yet I felt so much at home away from New Zealand that I was reluctant to return. Also, Frank Sargeson and I had talked of the advisability of my consulting a psychiatrist in London so that I might discover whether the New Zealand doctors had been correct in their diagnosis of schizophrenia. I knew I had not suffered from it. My claim, however, was naturally looked on with disbelief by almost everyone. Since the publication of my book of stories *The Lagoon*, John Forrest, my friend of distant student days, had written from America where he now lived. Not having seen me for eleven years, and unaware of my real story, my determination to live up to his expectation of me as 'kin to Hugo Wolf, Van Gogh', he also very likely had few doubts about the validity of the diagnosis. In answering his occasional letters I delivered with a casual touch, myself in my former role of supposed 'cleverness', 'difference', a dreamer of dreams, maker of fantasies. When John Forrest's inevitable 'Dear Everyone' letters arrived I smiled at my new maturity. With a touch of snobbery I had sometimes referred to him as 'My friend, the doctor in America.' I mention him because he had lately written to say that if I wished he could arrange an appointment with a doctor at the famous London hospital, the Maudsley.

El Americano

10

I had been told that spring came early in Las Baleares. Even so, its outbreak of blossom in early January encircled the island with a new bond of sweetness so excessive that it forced dark pleats of pain to be folded within the pleasure.

With the black-and-white beanflower filling acres of fields, the orchards pink and white with colours, never reproduced in paintings, that remain locked within certain flowers, with the spring wind warm, full of the scent of the wild flowers, the almond and avocado blossom, and the beanflowers, I prepared to tolerate the poetry I knew I would try to write in the midst of writing my novel. Often I remembered with a feeling of strangeness that I hadn't spoken English for three months, although I was aware of my English speech tucked away in the corner of my mouth with the key turned in the lock, but I did not realize how rusty with disuse were the key, the lock, and the speech until, arriving home from my walk one afternoon, I met Francesca who repeated excitedly, 'El Americano, El Americano,' while I listened mystified until I saw a tall brown-haired young man coming down the stairs into the sitting room.

He was equally startled to see me.

'Hi,' he said. 'I'm Edwin Mather. I've rented the studio upstairs. I'm a painter.'

I had to search for my English words. (*My* words indeed!)

'I live in the front room,' I said. 'I'm a writer.'

'I guess we share the kitchen and the john outside?'

El Americano. Just as Francesca had warned. Hadn't she told me that she left Algeria because Los Americanos came and took all the oil and perfume?

I felt sick with disappointment and a sense of betrayal for I believed I had rented the entire house and I could not understand how El Patron could now rent other rooms. Perhaps I had been mistaken. I had looked on Number Six Ignacio Riquer as *my place*, shared of course with El Patron and his family and Catalina and Francesca, but not with a *foreigner*, an American painter who spoke English! I felt hostile and unprotected as English thoughts and English words crowded into my head as into an auditorium, each ready to perform its role. There was no-one to appeal to. Number Six Ignacio Riquer had been *my place*.

I recovered a little. At least Edwin Mather would be living upstairs. He would share the house, though, the kitchen, the fire, the front door to the street, the hallway, the sitting room opening on to the patio, the lavatory on the patio, and I'd always be aware of a presence in the house and part of me would be tuned to that presence and distracted from my writing. I felt that the link between the world of living and of writing resembled a high wire needing intense relaxed concentration for the barefoot journey (on knives or featherbeds) between. In such a life the presence of others is a resented intrusion and becomes a welcome joyous diversion only when attention must be directed away from words, if only briefly, during times of travel and sickness.

On this first meeting Edwin and I, like candidates for a post which both had to accept (for he, too, may have thought he had rented the entire house) explained our presence in Ibiza—his funds were from a scholarship which he collected from Andorra where the money market was 'free'. Ignorant of the ways of international currency, I listened attentively as he advised me to change my foreign money in Andorra. He could arrange it, he said.

'Oh,' I said dubiously.

He showed me his studio upstairs, a large airy room with white stone walls, a skylight, and a door opening on to the roof with a panorama of the city, the fields, the ocean, and the mirror city. I felt suddenly disappointed in my restricting of my spirit of adventure — why had I never explored this upper storey of the house? Passing through the sitting room on my way to my bedroom I glanced always at the stone stairway as if it were a place forbidden, without realizing that it was I who had hung out the trespass warning, not aware that I was denying myself a richer view of Mirror City. This revelation of the panorama from the rooftop when I had spent day after day huddled in a rug in my chair in my room, my typewriter on the table before me, my gaze when it strayed from the typewriter fixed only on the mirror city across the harbour, had the effect of an earthquake, shifting my balance, opening depths beneath me, distorting yet enlarging my simple view, as simple as the stare of the blinkered horse I had seen harnessed to circle the well hour after hour, to draw water. No doubt the water was pure and sweet, bearing little relation to the routine of the imprisoned agent working at the well, but I was not so sure that what had appeared on my typewriter was so fresh and sparkling.

Suddenly also I was forced to make a new routine that took account of Edwin. Up early, lighting the fire, I now set aside Edwin's shaving and washing water, and by the time he was out of bed I had breakfasted and begun work. For the evening meal he usually ate with friends at a café or stayed home and cooked his specialty, French onion soup, or shared what was now my specialty, paella with *saffron* which I mention only because I took delight in thinking of myself as 'eating crocuses'. Edwin painted most of the day while I wrote and at times we'd have spontaneous or contrived meetings in the kitchen when he or I asked, 'Quiere el fuego?'

And soon the kitchen shelves became crowded with luxury food that set Catalina and Francesca aquiver with excitement. Edwin's first meeting with them prompted the remark, 'Who are those two old women wandering around prying into everything?'

I explained. Edwin appeared to be unsympathetic towards them while I, who felt that I 'understood' them, sprang to their defence, reminding him that they were poor and could not afford the kind of food he was buying and it was natural for them to help themselves from his bountiful larder.

'But they're wandering in and out all day.'

I told him they lived next door and our fire was their only means of cooking. They had one room, I told him, and they kept bantam hens on a small balcony off their bedroom. 'They might give you a fresh egg now and then,' I said.

He also complained, not unreasonably, about the light bulbs. Although his studio had natural light from the skylight he wanted to be able to paint whenever he wished and to read at night. (I was managing by lighting three or four candles at my table.) Edwin searched the town for new light bulbs which instantly blew the fuses in the house and brought rebuke from Fermin whom Edwin described as 'that interfering little guy with the violin. Have you heard the awful sounds he makes on that violin? I didn't know he would be using this house to practise!'

I pointed to the locked cupboard in the sitting room.

'He has carvings in there. The cupboard lights up when you open the door. He's a sensitive soul.'

Edwin's view of Francesca, Catalina, Fermin, depressed me for to me they were my new family who had looked after me and waited for my luggage to arrive and taught me to shop and cook, and when my three-month visa expired it had been Catalina who had taken me to the police station to introduce me as her friend the writer from Nueva Zelanda who needed her visa renewed. I felt that El Patron and his family needed protection against El Americano. He and his English or American language were the intruders.

For a time I could not adapt to what I saw as the destruction of my perfect world, and I still found writing difficult with a 'presence' in the house, yet gradually Edwin and I began to talk to each other about our work. Each day when he'd finished painting he'd invite me to his studio where he explained his morning's effort and talked about his ideas and art in general, his favourite artists, his life, and in return, although I did not discuss my current work, I lent him a copy of my novel, *Owls Do Cry*, which had now been published and had recently been at the correos when I collected my mail. Edwin liked *Owls Do Cry*. 'It should appear in the States,' he said. He knew someone in New York who worked for a publisher; perhaps he could send a copy there?

I said I'd 'see'.

Apart from professional talk and the phrase spoken often during the day, 'Quiere el fuego,' we lived our separate lives. Then one afternoon when I returned from my walk I was met by Catalina and Francesca in a state of excitement: Edwin had a woman visitor who'd be staying the night . . . in the same room . . . in the same bed. And that evening I met Dora, a flute-player from the mid-West, studying music in Paris. She was small, dainty, with black hair. She wore the 'right' clothes — black *pantalones* and sweater. I longed wistfully to be as full of secrets as she seemed to be, that would prompt a man to discover them, but for so long I had blocked all exits and entrances that I knew or felt that I was as sexless as a block of wood. I had smoothed myself away with veneers of protection.

That evening Edwin and Dora dined out while I, uneasily, with a nagging sense of loneliness and an unwillingness to return to my writing, prepared my self-sufficient meal, read for a while in the half-darkness, looked out dreamily at my Mirror City, then retired to bed. I heard Edwin and Dora come home, laughing and talking as they went up the stairs to his studio, and I felt the sudden unfriendly chill of being just myself and no-one else: not dainty but with legs that my sister had said were like footballer's legs, and wristbones that reminded me of railway sleepers.

Figuretti's

11

The next morning, Dora was gone even before I was up. She was catching a boat or plane to the mainland or the north. Edwin and I had a late breakfast and he talked casually of her as if she were just anyone. Catalina and Francesca could not stop talking about her, *la diabla*, who had stayed the night with El Americano, and the bedsheets had to be washed and what a disgrace. A female devil! They turned to me, 'You're not like her, you're not a female devil. Los Americanos!'

I knew I had played that role before — as a child at home, at school, at university and college: the keeper of the rules, the 'good' person delivered from evil, never led into temptation. Where then the praise had given me a feeling of syrupy self-complacence, now it gave little satisfaction for in the arithmetic of my thirty-two years it was now a subtraction from rather than an addition to my self-esteem.

For a while my life returned more or less to its usual routine. Then one evening when I was in my room typing I heard the sound of voices in the kitchen, men's voices punctuated by hearty laughter, and with the pretext of fetching hot water, I went to satisfy my curiosity and found Edwin and a friend whom he introduced as *Bernard* whose thirty-fourth birthday they were celebrating. I said hello (unable to bring myself to use what I thought of as that ridiculous 'Hi!'), shared a toast with a glass of rosé (the best on the island, according to Bernard), and then, explaining that I had work to do, I returned to my room, and as I left, I heard Edwin say, 'Janet has had a book published.'

Later, in bed, I still heard their laughter grown slightly drunken now as the hours passed. I thought Bernard's laughter was the most joyous I had ever heard. The sound seemed to have the right assembly to connect with a jagged shape inside my heart. I could not otherwise explain the delight of listening to his laughter.

The next morning, a blue and white and green spring morning, leaving my work untouched and with a surge of domesticity, I prepared to cook the marmalade from the recipe Edwin had cut from the *Observer*, and the blood-tinged fruit was bubbling in the big pan Catalina lent me, and I was leaning over the pan, stirring the golden blood-streaked syrupy liquid when the door opened and Bernard walked in.

'Hi,' he said. 'I couldn't work this morning. I thought I'd take a walk. Care to come?'

I felt nervous. 'What work do you do?' I asked, remembering that Edwin had said something about Bernard helping to bring Freud into Spain by working on the oil pipeline in Northern Spain.

'Back home, I'm a history professor. I was working on the pipeline until I fell off a horse and broke my arm — it's healing now. I'm really a poet. I've written several poems since I've been on the island.'

He was of medium build with fair hair, grey eyes, and a rich voice that sounded like chords of music to my already enchanted ears. I thought his eyes, intent in their gaze, looked slightly glazed and mad: in my innocence it never occurred to me that he might have been taking drugs. He watched while I poured the marmalade into the six prepared jars, and now and then when I leaned forward I saw him staring down my dress at my breasts. He kept staring at them. He stared at me, too, with his bright, mad-looking eyes.

We talked of ourselves.

'I couldn't work either,' I said. 'This beautiful day.'

'Let's go for a walk along the beach past Figuretti's.'

'Figuretti's?'

'Yes. Don't you know Figuretti's?'

I said no, I didn't, and he didn't explain and during the rest of my stay on the island I never discovered the nature or meaning of

Figuretti's. At times I thought it was a café on the beach, then I thought it must be a bay, then a patch of sky, for in the weeks that followed Bernard and others I came to know would say, 'Figuretti's is beautiful today,' or 'It's just past Figuretti's,' or 'When I first went to Figuretti's.' Once, Bernard pointed to a café, a group of buildings, the church, the sky, 'Look,' he said in a satisfied tone. 'There's Figuretti's.'

Strangely, I cherished my ignorance and never inquired.

I sealed the last jar of marmalade and set the six in a row on the table. Edwin will be pleased, I thought, listening in vain for the sound of him working in his studio, and I wished that I lived in the days of pen and quill when authors, too, were silent workers and none knew, listening, what sound of words they might be mixing and stirring and applying to the parchment or paper.

'Edwin is busy,' I murmured.

We walked along the narrow streets, uphill through a grove of tall cacti with their calloused spiked palms upward. Bernard pointed to the entrances of the caves where some Ibicencans lived. I was aware of myself now making another journey, a first, as I had when Ben and I searched London for a chess set that in spite of the occasional surfacing of dreams and desires, remained a literal chess set on which to play a real game of chess. This beach walk with Bernard was recognized by us as an intention like the preliminary movement that birds make when determining their final flight. Bernard and I also laughed and talked and quoted our favourite poets (I was slightly disappointed when he quoted Kipling's 'Gunga Din'), but I was again entranced with him when I learned that he spoke fluent French and Spanish and at once I drew out my favourite quotations, like confections being cooked, shaped and set for tasting. Picture, then, a woman of thirty-two, fresh-complexioned, blue-eyed, dressed in a blue jersey 'sack' which Edwin (a painter who should know) said was a 'beautiful colour', and Roman sandals. (Frank Sargeson always wore Roman sandals in summer. He had only to say to me, 'Roman sandals are best and cheapest for summer. You need Roman sandals,' for me to make Roman sandals part of my spring and summer existence wherever in the world I might be living.) Picture me by the 'blue Mediterranean' beginning to quote a fable learned years ago, quoting to share my pleasure in the verse and to show my cleverness in remembering it,

Maître Corbeau, sur un arbre perché,
Tenait en son bec un fromage.
Maître Renard, par l'odeur alléché,
Lui tint à peu près ce langage:
Hé! bonjour monsieur du Corbeau.
Que vous êtes joli! que vous me semblez beau . . .

and then, done with La Fontaine, turning for good measure to Alphonse Daudet, I shook the dust from 'Si vous avez jamais passé la nuit à la belle étoile, vous savez qu'à l'heure où nous dormons un monde mystérieux s'éville dans le solitude et le silence. Alors le source chante bien plus clair et il y a dans l'air les frôlements, les bruits imperceptibles si l'on entendit l'herbe pousser, la branche grandir . . .' followed by a helping of Victor Hugo, 'C'est pour renaître ailleurs qu'ici bas on succombe . . . '

I had thus hinted at my supposed cleverness and now it was Bernard's turn to impress me.

'What about Auden?' he said.

I was rapturous. 'Oh! Auden!'

I began, 'He disappeared in the dead of winter/The brooks were frozen . . . '

Follow, poet, follow right
To the bottom of the night.
With your unconstraining voice
Still persuade us to rejoice . . .

Bernard responded with a quote from Edna St Vincent Millay while I listened with polite attention, snobbishly aware that *my* poets were 'better' than his, and wishing he would quote long passages of Yeats as I tried to preserve my image of his perfection from my realistic impulse to destroy what I had created from the day, the circumstance, and the person who talked longingly of the mysterious Figuretti's. We walked on, our spirits rising as we looked about us at the sea, the sky, and smelled the beanflowers, the almond blossom and the innumerable unnamed flowers growing everywhere in an everlasting springtime.

We passed a gaunt cow grazing at the end of its tethering rope, its circle of earth bare of grass, and with a gesture of magnanimity towards the world, Bernard withdrew the post and led the cow to a new pasture, but after he had sunk the post in the earth he picked up a stick and struck the cow's hide sharply twice in a burst of unprovoked anger that reminded me of the gesture of the pale physicist assaulting the tortoise on the lawn at Clapham Common. Again I fought to mantle and not to dismantle the perfection of the Ibicencan day.

We walked on. The light wind blew a bundle of grass across the sand to the water.

'Look,' Bernard cried with delight. 'Tumbleweed! Do you know tumbleweed?'

Ashamed, I said I had believed that tumbleweed was a roaming cowboy. With my childhood of Western films my mind turned easily to Texas, New Mexico, Arizona and their flora and fauna and the cowboy songs I used to sing, among them

Drifting along with the tumbling tumbleweed . . .

My response was ecstatic. So this was tumbleweed! I watched as the bundle of dry grass, its roots enclosing itself, rolled on and on towards the sea where it stopped and partly propelling itself, partly in the hand of the wind, it zigzagged along the shore, never pausing to rest or take root. Although I did not want to indulge in anthropomorphism or pathetic fallacy I did invest in the tumbleweed a power of detachment, of protective isolation: I looked sympathetically on it. We had walked the length of the beach passing on the way the white stone villa Bernard had rented, a few yards from the water. We talked of ourselves and our lives and when Bernard asked if I were married I said no, but, unwilling to reveal myself as sexually but not technically a virgin, I gave dark hints of liaisons of former days.

Bernard had married at an early age and was now separated.

I had no-one special, I said. I had one or two men friends but I was so busy with my writing that I had little time or inclination for affairs of the heart.

My attempt at mystery amused Bernard. He laughed heartily and each time he laughed I felt within me a reverberation of his laughter as if I were a vast empty palace awaiting the guests and the feast.

We climbed the hill at the far end of the beach overlooking a triangular sea and the neatly terraced land with every inch cultivated to yield its fruit. We spread our picnic on the grass and ate and drank and talked and as we looked down at the fields and the sea, I stood with his arm encircling my waist. We had been away for hours. It was growing dark.

'Let's go to my villa,' Bernard said, 'and build a log fire.'

Hand in hand we retraced our steps along the beach to the white stone villa. A villa on the beach! The fairytale image of a life lived like a shellfish within reach of the sea and within sight of the tumbleweed that now took its place as a special plant beside my loved matagouri!

When Bernard and I had eaten a meal and were sitting in the twilight beside a blazing log fire, enacting a cliché drawn from all the *True Romance* magazines I had read in my girlhood, I felt the satisfaction of having yet another first experience — merely sitting, talking of interesting matters as well as exchanging hints of feeling, underlining, signing an invisible contract without speaking of it, in an atmosphere of mutual excitement. I, unlike Bernard, was new to seduction.

The night wind from the Mediterranean brought a chill into the room and I reached to shut the window. Bernard leaned forward, gripped me tightly around my waist, pressing our bodies close. I struggled free.

'Oh no,' I said primly. 'I've only just met you. I don't know you. I don't believe in . . . I mean I've just met you.'

Then, adopting a calm, reasoned objective approach, I not only successfully extinguished the spark but washed it over, becoming my own sea, with a dampening regret; and no store of kindling in sight.

For a while, then, we talked, still excitedly exchanging details of our lives, our beliefs, opinions, all punctuated inevitably by romantic quotes from poetry.

It was early morning when we walked along the cobbled streets towards Ignacio Riquer and as we stood outside 'my' house, he again clasped me tightly while his practised hands sought the 'right' places, and he kissed me until I responded and we stood, breathless, in the dark street. I then freed myself, said a prim goodnight, and went inside to my room, with my body feeling as if still enclosed by him in an embrace that lingered all night, like a phantom, and when it began to recede like a slowly vanishing dream, I willed it to return.

I spent a restless few days.

'I don't hear your typewriter,' Edwin said in a complaining tone as if the sound of my typewriter were a necessary accompaniment to his own working; and it may have been, for a state of restlessness can be infectious and any departure from an artist's planned routine can be a trigger to anarchy as the ideas, looking in, find nowhere to come home to.

'Aren't you working these days?'

I 'laughed lightly' (as I had read it described in novels when laughter is heaviest and most melancholy) for like the place on earth where the giant has lain, the memory of Bernard left its deep print, and, waking one morning with a haunting thought that I (shy, in my thirty-third year, travelling overseas to 'broaden my experience') might never have another such experience, I dressed, prepared Edwin's shaving water, then walked out along the street towards the hill and the sea and Bernard's villa. I stopped at the *pastelria* to buy breakfast cakes. I walked through the grove of tall cactus trees by the white windowless houses and the caves. I came to the beach, the 'blue Mediterranean where he lay lulled by the coil of the crystalline streams.'

I looked for tumbleweed but saw none.

I knocked on the door of Bernard's villa.

He was not surprised to see me. He was wearing a dressing-gown and had a scrap of paper in his hand.

'I've been writing a poem,' he said. 'About spring in Ohio.'

He began to read, 'Only spring in Ohio . . . '

I thought it was a slight, almost a nothing poem, and when he had finished reading it I murmured, 'Oh. Spring in Ohio. It must be lovely.'

'It is. It's like no other springtime. You wake one morning and it's there. The suddenness of Ibicencan spring reminds me of it.'

'Spring in Ohio,' I murmured fatuously, looking shy when Bernard turned his attention from his poem to me.

'I haven't had breakfast yet,' he said. 'I write best on an empty stomach.'

It reminded me of an old radio joke and I wanted to snigger but I thrust my bag of breakfast cakes on the table and said, 'I brought your breakfast.'

And so we sat facing each other, eating our breakfast cakes and continuing our conversation where it had lapsed several evenings since, punctuating our prose with quotes of our favourite poems with each silently judging the poetic taste of the other until, our breakfast over, we sat on the sofa facing the wide window looking out at the beach. The Mediterranean, I thought to myself, aware that I had moved into a permanent cliché.

And then Bernard was slowly undressing me and I was unbuttoning his buttons and we both knew this was the reason for my visit. Naked, we went to the bedroom to the big double bed while the sea hushed and washed and hushed outside and the morning sun dazzled and glittered in the room. Bernard was about to draw the curtains when I said, thinking I sounded very experienced, and remembering a sentence from the book *Meeting and Mating* that my sisters and I had studied years ago, 'It is a good idea to make love in daylight,' casually as if I knew it all.

I lay on the bed. I stared at Bernard's large erected penis. I did not dare say that this was the first time I had been with a naked man. I continued to stare at the red-roofed dovecote full of white doves ready to fly into the sky and never return; and I was the sky; and how strange that was, I, with all my conversation during our walk, about the 'men in my life' was having a first experience and only I knew. And there was Bernard suddenly two beings, himself, and the manikin that resembled a dovecote. I felt the sadness and finality of being in the midst of a *True Romance* ('then he . . . then I . . . ') in a white stone villa by the Mediterranean.

Bernard then went to the bathroom and returned with the dovecote dressed in a condom while a vague unhappiness came over me as I asked myself, 'Why is he so prepared, carrying them about like indigestion tablets?' I quelled my momentary chill: I did not want to forgo my new experience. Oh why, I thought, must I touch up my feelings to make them acceptably *love* as it should be without doubts and suspicions. And thus I apply cosmetics to what may be already a corpse?

We spent the morning lovemaking. In spite of my reading in the subject, I, limited in my knowledge to the 'missionary' act, suffered or enjoyed shocks and surprises that were lessened by the addicting sensations. Besides, I felt I could not undo my lies about myself as 'experienced'. I, who supposed I was always searching for the 'truth', was I now searching for the truth within a lie? I knew the lies were those of vanity and cowardice, of unwillingness to see my life as it had been and not as I supposed or hoped it might have been.

In the afternoon, newly entwined in a strong swiftly sealed bond, arms around each other, hands clasped tightly, we walked out in the daylight through the streets of the town. We passed Figuretti's.

'There's Figuretti's,' Bernard said while I stared about me at the mysterious world of sky, stone, sand, sea.

'Figuretti's,' I repeated as if it were a game, a contest I had engaged in all my life and could never know the answers.

We came to the Post Office where I found a parcel waiting for me. From England. Who could have sent it?

Later, at the villa, we opened the parcel to find four tins of corned beef from Patrick Reilly.

And a letter that ended, 'I hope you are still fancy free.'

I savoured the feeling of transgressing as Bernard and I lay in bed making love and later eating our corned beef and French loaf.

From that day I spent every night and much of the day at Bernard's villa. I'd steal home at breakfast time, trying to keep up the pretence of the innocent *escritora* from Nueva Zelanda and knowing I had failed when I saw the disappointment in the eyes of both Catalina and Francesca when I met them one morning as I came in the door.

'El Americano?' Francesca questioned with a sly smile. 'Mucho dinero?'

I lapsed into my mixture of French and Spanish.

'No sé,' I said coolly. 'Peut-être.'

It was generally accepted, then, that all Americans were rich, chiefly because they appeared to take for granted and buy the most costly food and goods. Even Edwin, with his scholarship, lived in luxury with purchases beyond the reach of Catalina, Francesca and myself. And there was Bernard living in his 'villa by the Mediterranean'! I could sense the subtle shift in the feelings of Catalina and Francesca towards me; I was no longer the bewildered Janetta all alone, waiting for her luggage and her typewriter; I had become, not without a sense of triumph for myself as well as a feeling of loss, one of the female devils, and, being one, I knew I had now sacrificed the rare pleasure of again being invited to Catalina's and Francesca's tiny apartment to share, say, a fiesta party, sitting around the table laughing and talking while the brazier burned beneath.

Now, I had joined Los Americanos. I was Bernard's 'woman'.

Bernard and I called on other Americans, many of them exiles from the McCarthy regime — the film director turned painter who had built himself a villa in Ibiza and who conducted us through his personal gallery of the American Civil War where each of the portraits of the Generals were portraits of himself. We attended recitals of music and poetry at the French Institute. We wined and dined with Edwin's and Bernard's friends, mostly Americans, with the men and women living with their chosen partners in the sensuous sensual kind of luxury enjoyed by the lotus eaters. Now and then I found myself in alarming situations—the time I arrived at a dinner party to discover I was the only guest while my host, a stranger, sitting at the far end of the table suddenly collapsed with malaria and I wondered as I helped him to his bedroom and undressed him if his sickness was a version of the 'etchings' we had often laughed about in our girlhood. He was genuinely ill. Aware that I was indeed fulfilling the purpose of my literary grant by 'broadening my experience', I sat all night by his bed, preparing and feeding him medicine.

During our calls on the Americans I learned much from what was said and unsaid. I heard of the mechanics of drug-running. I was not aware that anyone I knew was drug-trafficking or taking but my innocence in this was so complete that I wonder now if I misread signs or neglected to notice them. I simply listened, fascinated by all the stories as if I were a child allowed to stay up late to listen to the exploits of the grown-up world.

I was unable to ignore some real intimations of the future of others and in turn to wonder about my own risks when I heard that Barbara, a painter living and painting happily with Greg, another painter, was suddenly alone, in distress. Greg had gone to Paris and would not be returning and people were asking Barbara how would she manage when the baby was born. Would she stay on the island? How would she provide for herself? Would she return to America to have the baby or would she choose not to have it? There was still time . . . someone knew someone who knew someone . . . Everyone felt sorry for Barbara. It had happened to others, too, they said.

On one of my rare meetings with Edwin at Ignacio Riquer when I murmured out of habit our classic phrase of—centuries ago, in my life—'Quiere el fuego?' he replied with, 'I hope you know what you're doing?'

'Of course I do,' I said.

'But what about your writing? I never hear your typewriter these days. What has happened?'

'Well . . . '

Bernard occupied my mind and my body. We explored the island, hiring bicycles and spending the day on remote beaches. We talked and quoted and sang and made love. Once, we visited his friends on a yacht in the harbour (Mirror City!). Their supply of guns frightened me.

Then one night when we were in bed Bernard said, dismayed, 'I've run out of supplies. I meant to get some.'

I felt distaste for his concern. In such moments one does not care about such things.

'What does it matter?' I said recklessly.

Later, I said dreamily, 'What if I do have a baby?'

Bernard's reply shocked me.

'That would be terrible,' he said

He meant it. That would be terrible. His words haunted me with a reality that until then had been unable to reach me. A baby, a loving replica of Bernard and me; a gift from Bernard for whom I'd felt a determined kind of love that, during the past weeks as soon as there were signs of disarray, I had quickly straightened and smoothed to preserve in perfection—wasn't a baby the fulfillment of our love?

His words, 'That would be terrible,' effectively destroyed that perfect love. Quite suddenly the place on earth marked—as I thought indelibly—by the giant resumed its former shape and growth. I felt my life, like the grass, resuming its place, responding to sun and light and wind: my longing and love and passion for Bernard were gone. His cold words, 'That would be terrible. A baby would be terrible,' how could he have thought and spoken them? A baby would be terrible.

That night was the last I spent at the villa. I returned to live and write in my room at Calle Ignacio Riquer. I found a key for the front door and locked it and refused to answer when Bernard called. Edwin and I returned to our routine of painting and writing and each afternoon I went to his studio to see his morning's work. He had named one of his paintings 'The Street Where the Children Don't Play Anymore'.

'Remember?' he said.

I remembered. We had been walking late through the streets while someone played the flute and the flute-notes fell sharp as broken cobblestones, glittering in the moonlight and the children who had been playing all day in the street had long since vanished.

'It's like a street where the children don't play any more,' I said.

Then one day Edwin told me that Bernard was leaving the island. I was missing him. We had nested in each other and there's no warmer nest than skin.

The day Bernard left, I gave Edwin a bunch of wild flowers to take to him at the ship.

75

Catalina and Francesca were both pleased to learn that El Americano had gone.

'Los Americanos,' they said. 'They disturb everything. Everywhere. Even the light.'

And that was true, for Edwin was in disgrace again having blown the electric fuses with his high-powered lamps.

'They disturb the light,' Francesca said. 'And make everything dark.'

I stayed six more weeks in Ibiza. Not being with Bernard hurt more than I had supposed it would for he had taken over my life and my self and now, in his absence, searching the empty places, I found only a blank uninhabited darkness with fleeting glimpses of Bernard. My love had been awakened partly through my deliberate engineering of my feelings and partly through my delight in the sound of Bernard's laughter. I had nurtured the love and even in the short period I had known it, its complexity, its light absorbed everything I knew or felt or had been or would be.

True Romance indeed! So much for poetry and music! I was beginning to suspect that I might be pregnant. I was overtaken by an alarm that did not quite match my image of perfect love. Also, my money would not last for ever. Edwin, whom I did not tell of my possible plight but who knew my funds were low, suggested I might try living in Andorra, the 'free' money-market he had spoken of before. He sensed that Ibiza had become an intolerable place for me — Ibiza, my island now in its warm balm of blossom with the interior and the gentle hills shining with the forests of light-green pine trees, their branches tipped a glossier lighter green with new growth — Ibiza was suddenly changed, steeped in my own feelings, destroyed by my glance. Where before my surroundings (I supposed) had existed in their own right, the sky and the sea and the weather and the Mirror City, and I too had existed in my own right, with the island and its features as my companions, now all suffered an effect, not the Midas touch but the touch of ash: I could almost see the trees decaying, the olive blossoms withering; also, I was invaded by knowing others on the island, I was no longer alone, creator and preserver of my world, in harmony with other worlds because I could interpret them as I wished: I was tasting the sour and bitter of absence and lost pleasure, bound to a magnet of reality.

(When autumn is' over and the leaves have fallen from the trees with only the dark evergreens retaining their bulk which is at once a shelter and an obstacle to the passage of light, we see that we have never been alone in the forest. Shapes of houses emerge, people going about their daily lives; there's a new perspective of distance, a discovery of horizons one could never see during spring and summer and guess at only, throughout autumn. Look at those tall chimneys rising from fires we never knew were lit but that still burn, fuelled in secret! Look at the newly revealed paths! Now I, more clearly looking through this and that world and its seasons become also more clearly looked at. My own surroundings lose their camouflage; I myself lose my camouflage. There is even the possibility of nests, new or abandoned, in my own tree!)

Andorra

12

I left Ibiza on a grey day when the Mediterranean was whipped mountainously by a gale into waves thirty feet high and I and the other passengers had to be helped on board the violently tossing ferry. There was a kind of recklessness, an embracing of doom in the way I ignored what would formerly have terrified me. I said goodbye to Edwin, faithful Edwin who still hoped to see *Owls Do Cry* published in New York. I then went at once to my cabin and was seasick all night and in the morning, in the glassy calm when the ship, scarcely moving, berthed at Barcelona, I collected my suitcases, my green haversack, and grasping these and my bulky Traveller's Joy handbag, I sat in a classically forlorn pose, on an upturned suitcase, on Barcelona wharf as I recovered from my seasickness and wondered where to go and what to do. I knew only that my *destination* was Andorra.

Later, I found a room in a small hotel and as I walked into the hallway and smelled the pervading smell of olives and olive oil, I felt a wave of homesickness for Ibiza, Catalina, Francesca, Fermin, José, all my Ibicencan family and myself as the innocent *escritora* with the quiet uncomplicated daily chores and the simple stack of typing paper and the communion with Mirror City.

And now it was Bernard whose presence stayed, like a phantom. He was there beside me, around, within me. Hearing his laughter in the street I'd look out to see a stranger laughing and talking among strangers.

The next morning I was told that no buses travelled to Andorra at that time of year. It was still winter on the mainland and the months of Ibicencan spring were like a mirage, a dream remembered in the cold wind of Barcelona. The roads to Andorra were impassable except for one used by private cars. I could hire a taxi, someone suggested.

The taxi was cheap. I could not believe that I, a New Zealander who never went anywhere by taxi, was travelling late that morning from Barcelona to Andorra with two other passengers, through the villages of northern Spain, past the fields and ancient monasteries and the miles of red earth. The other passengers soon left the minibus, for such it was, leaving me marvelling alone at the small villages growing like dark-red fruit and flowers out of the earth, or like old wounds, still open in places, covered with congealed blood that beneath the brilliant blue sky were unrelieved by the usual benison of green. I tried to seize and hold the memory of those villages for I knew that this would perhaps be my only journey through northern Spain. I knew also that whatever I remembered I would see the country's wounds opening as in the Civil War and I'd think of my Ibicencan friends and Fermin pointing to the place of the executions beside the Stations of the Cross.

Soon the bus began its ascent through the foothills of the Pyrenees where the light became choked suddenly by the forests of dark green pines, almost black in the afternoon. The contrast between the gently light-green trees of Ibiza, their foliage soft, clouded, sometimes yellow in the falling sunlight, and the stark black of the northern trees against the snow seemed to be part of the natural regression from southern spring to northern winter and in tune with the mood of the inescapable present that sooner or later besets a woman of thirty-two who is alone and may be pregnant. (Undoubtedly during that journey I performed an exercise in emotional pollution by transposing the outward to the inward scene, back and forth until I might have believed that I became the dark winter-embraced pine tree.)

By late afternoon we had arrived at the village of Andorra La Vella where I unloaded my increasingly burdensome luggage, paid the

79

driver, and once again sat on an upturned suitcase while I pondered my next move. I had supposed that Andorra would be a large town of the principality, but here was a village square lined with buildings and, beyond, the mountains. I therefore began to walk along the street and I had just turned a corner on the road out of town when I met a young man.

'Por favor,' I said. 'Quiero una habitacion.'

Without replying at first he beckoned me to follow him until we came to a carload of workmen leaving Andorra for their homes in other villages. The young man, Carlos, explained that he would take me to his home in Les Escaldes where he was sure his wife and he could give me a room.

'Come with me,' he said.

A short drive away, at Les Escaldes, Carlos and I left the car and walked through the main street towards the river, a roaring mountain torrent that washed at the basement walls of the tenement buildings lining its banks. We climbed the narrow stairs of one such building to the third floor, an apartment overlooking the street where Carlos, his wife Donna, their two children, six-year-old Antoine and four-year-old Xavier lived, and as Carlos was explaining to Donna that I was hoping to find *una habitacion* with them, the children, shy, large-eyed, clung to their mother's skirt and stared at me. The stare changed to angry bewilderment when they learned that their bedroom was no longer their bedroom, but Mama's and Papa's also, while I was to sleep in Mama's and Papa's room, in the big double bed with the feather mattress. I did not learn at once of my disruption of the family's sleeping arrangements but I soon understood that, struggling in poverty, they were grateful for extra pesetas. The remaining small bedroom was rented to another lodger, El Vici Mario, whom I met for the first time that evening.

The other rooms were a tiny kitchen, a lavatory with a washbasin and two taps, hot and cold, with only the cold giving water as the town's hot water, drawn from hot springs in the mountains, could be freely used at the basins and taps in the square and the municipal bathing and washing house.

My room looked on to the street, closely overlooked by the snow-covered Pyrenees, and the night air in the room tasted of snow and was so cold that it had the effect of pain, not endless, but mingled with the pleasurable anticipation of daylight and, perhaps, the sun's warmth. I snuggled into my featherbed like a bird in its nest with the mattress heaped around me, and there I tried to plan a future that included a child, for it was almost certain that I was pregnant. I remembered how my small eight-year-old friend, Poppy, had said that if Hollywood stars didn't want their babies they drank gin or ate quinine or ran up and down mountains . . . well, I was in the Pyrenees, wasn't I? How had Poppy collected such folklore? And why did I think so swiftly of childhood solutions? I knew that in hospital I'd had a serious enduring lesson on what may happen when one person in a group or community has power to decide the life or death of others, and giving myself such a right was abhorrent. Yet, trying to enter the nearer reality, I became trapped in it. I did hurry up and down the slopes of the Pyrenees. I also swallowed quinine tablets. At the same time, I prepared for the baby so as to clothe and warm it. I bought wool, knitting needles, a French book of instructions (explaining, 'ma soeur . . . son bébé . . .') and I began knitting for 'le premier âge' from the section 'de la naissance à trois mois . . . pour tous les soins du bébé . . . ensemble d'exécution simple et rapide . . .' I knitted a tiny matinée jacket and bootees, placing them neatly in the bottom of my suitcase.

Another month passed. I had begun to fit in with the family's routine, each morning taking the tin bucket along the street, over the ancient stone bridge to the dairy for the day's milk, returning in time to share breakfast with the children, now up and dressed, and El Vici Mario and Donna and Carlos. We sat around the table with the big bowl of bread and milk in the centre while each fed from the bowl and passed it to the next person. Then Xavier and Antoine left for the Spanish school (Andorra had both Spanish and French schools). Even at four, Xavier was reading in the first sentence of his first book, of earliest violence — 'Cain mató a su hermano Abel . . .'

During the day when Carlos and El Vici and the children had gone, Donna and I talked about 'this and that' — the children, Carlos, El Vici, how hard it was to earn a living during the winter when there was little work for a carpenter, and how Carlos therefore earned money during the winter by waiting at a restaurant on Sunday evenings, bringing home wages that he could not count for he could neither read nor write nor calculate, and that Donna who had been to school counted for him, trying to teach him by arranging coloured counters with the coins on the dining room table. This was why it was important, she said, for the children to go to school each day in all weathers; and perhaps one day the family might emigrate to Canada to start a new life. Their neighbours in the apartment opposite, overlooking the river, were emigrating to Canada. The woman's husband had left ten months ago promising to send the fare for his wife and children when he had earned enough money and found a permanent place to live. He'd written at first, and he'd even sent money for the housekeeping, but for months there had been no word from him and sometimes Lola had cried wondering what would become of her and the three *crios*.

In the afternoons and evenings I'd tell the children stories using both the French and Spanish versions of 'Once upon a time'—'Il y avait une fois' and 'Hay en tiempos muy remotos . . . ' phrases that always transport me to the mirror world like the Mirror City where civilizations live their lives under the light of the imagination instead of the sun. Lured always by that world and by the fascination of trying to describe it in words that may not even exist for accurate description, from a limited vocabulary, I realized increasingly the extent of its treasure, discovered during visits to the Mirror City where the great artists had lived and returned to describe what they had seen and felt and known. I knew that some had visited and never returned. And here was I with yet another key to the city—'Hay en tiempos muy remotos', an entrance through the past to the present and the future with stories picked like flowers from the wayside as the traveller moves to and from the City.

As in Ibiza, I became one of the family in Les Escaldes. On Sundays, wearing my black mantilla, I went to church with the family. On Sunday evenings we went to the local cinema where we watched an American film, usually a Western, with Spanish subtitles. And while in the morning I tried to type my book, I was becoming more worried about the pregnancy and myself as the mother of a child: occasionally I was happy, thinking I'd have a replica of Bernard, picturing a boy with Bernard's face and build and laugh, or a girl with his eyes; while of myself reproduced I could see only another fuzzily red-haired Shirley Temple-dimpled child as I had been and I could not imagine Bernard's contribution to another myself. Perhaps, I thought, our grandparents might emerge, effectively cancelling or setting aside our characteristics, or heredity might reach further into the past to retrieve some abandoned trait waiting like a railway coach on a siding to be returned to the main line.

Such romantic dreams were soon dismissed as I recklessly wandered in the mountains, climbing steep slopes, and vaguely wondering about

the signs, *Perigo, Danger, Avalanches*. I climbed to the warm lake nestled
in the peaks, and I sat gazing down at the dark pines below the
snowline, and again I thought of the pines of Ibiza 'que el corazon
venera' contrasting them with the dark grief-bowed heads of the pines
of Andorra. I passed villages of stone that seemed to be growing out
of the rock, huge barns full of cattle, the smell of their manure lingering
around the entrance but freezing to nothingness in the mountain breath
of the snow. Soon, I was told, the sheep would be driven home through
the passes from France where they spent each winter. I learned much
about these mountain passes from El Vici who knew the routes by
heart and who earned his living, in winter, both as a smuggler and
a guide. My naiveté was such that El Vici's smuggling gave him a
romantic aura: I never wondered about the nature of the goods
smuggled: I simply imagined a group of wild-looking men, El Vici
among them, trundling packhorses laden with boxes of contraband
across the rugged mountain passes.

After my daily walk I swallowed my quinine tablet as I hoped and
denied my hope and grew increasingly fearful and pleased at my
condition. It was the need for light that brought a solution to the
problem. Although Andorra, unlike Ibiza, had plentiful electricity
from the mountain rivers, the inhabitants like Carlos and Donna were
too poor to use it and therefore, as in Ibiza, the electric light bulbs
were too dim for reading and writing. As Edwin had done in Ibiza
(El Americano who 'killed' the light), as Francesca described him, I
bought a bulb of higher wattage and standing on a chair, and reaching
to change the light to a higher intensity, I became dizzy and sick and
fell, and blood flowed reminding me of that first time it had flowed,
in the daffodil, snow, World War and birthday time in Oamaru. The
blood was bulky. I collected it in a towel and flushed it down the
lavatory, pulling the chain several times before it shredded (a quick
horror-filled glance told me) and vanished.

Weak and sick I lay in my featherbed and looked at the snow on
the mountains.

'You're very pale,' Donna said that evening.

'It's one of those days,' I said.

She smiled, recognizing that we were two women in a male
household. I did not realize until the baby had gone that I had accepted
it and was preparing for it. I knew a feeling that was stronger than
regret but not as intense as bereavement, a no-woman's land of feeling
where a marvellous sense of freedom sprang up beside hate for myself,

longing for Bernard and what he had given me and never knew, sadness for a lost path, vanishings, with the sense of freedom and the prospect of living a new life in Mirror City, triumphing like the rankest, strongest, most pungent weeds that yet carry exquisite flowers, outgrowing the accepted flowers in no-woman's land.

The physical loss, like widowhood, of Bernard and the loss of the tiny envelope of growth, his 'share', made me turn naturally to accept El Vici's offered company, urged by the delighted Donna and Carlos who already had plans to see us married in the new church. My few days' sickness aroused less attention because the two boys had developed chickenpox and were kept home from school in their darkened room and given drinks of *tisane*.

And in my newly clarified and fused and perhaps con-fused state I accepted El Vici's invitation to go with him for a picnic in the mountains, and so one morning, aware of the approval of Carlos and Donna and of the glances of El Vici's friends along the street, we set out with our picnic along the mountain paths towards the snowline. I had learned that El Vici had been a Resistance worker during the war, later a prisoner in a French concentration camp, and after the war he came to live in Andorra as his knowledge of the mountain pathways was intimate and detailed; in the autumn he picked grapes in the south of France or worked in a fur shop in the south. Like many Italians he was a skilled bicycle racer and so had brought his wonderful blue and white bicycle to Andorra where it was kept in his bedroom, for although he did not ride it, he polished it, oiled it, and turned it upside down on the landing while he spun the wheels and fiddled with the gears. He had given me this information about himself in French which, with Italian and Spanish, he spoke fluently.

I, always an admirer of those with a gift for language, was prepared to like this tall handsome man. I admired his fight against the Fascists led by Il Duce, Mussolini, I sympathized with his suffering and torture in a concentration camp; the fact, however, that I could not accept his wearing of two-tone black and white shoes, and particularly his wearing them in the photograph he gave me, is more a comment on me and the influence of my early life than upon the character of El Vici. In my past and lost world any man wearing 'two-tone' shoes was a 'spiv', a 'lounge lizard', possibly a gangster.

As we walked towards the snow El Vici pointed out landmarks and we talked in French although occasionally we would speak Spanish. We stopped a few yards from the snow that I, enraptured always by snow, heralded with quotes from French poetry in what seemed to me to be an alarming, even a pathetic, repetition of my first walk in Ibiza with Bernard. I felt that I was playing an old record, perhaps my only one, and I thought, would it always be like this, in these circumstances, up and down the same worn pathways of the brain?

As I spread the food on the bare patch of rock, El Vici told how he had been born and brought up in Milano, how his father was a quiet man and his mother was huge in build (he spread his hands apart to depict the width of his mother). He explained that he'd not had 'la bonne chance' with women.

As we began to eat our salami and bread and drink our wine, he suddenly leaned forward to grab at my breasts. I, the prim young woman again, struggled free.

'Oh no,' I said, adopting the manner of a counsellor on affairs of the heart. 'Let's talk about this.' I didn't kiss and cuddle those I didn't know well, I said.

'But you have come walking in the mountains with me,' El Vici protested. 'No woman goes walking in the mountains with a man unless they wish to be lovers.' Women did not go out alone as I did, walking and walking by the river, through the streets, in the mountains. In future, he said, someone should walk with me. He would walk with me and when he was working, Donna and Carlos and the children would escort me. I was Andorran now, he said. Andorra was my home.

El Vici's feelings were more serious than I had gauged. After the day of the picnic he made sure that I did not walk alone, and as it was now the beginning of the Andorran spring, although the road into France was still closed, the mountain flowers were coming into bloom and Donna and the children and I went picking flowers — white violets, primroses, freesias, lilies, their scent still frozen within them by the snowfilled air. I still managed to have my solitary walks, sometimes following the path of the Andorra river or walking into Andorra La Vella to collect parcels sent by Patrick Reilly from England — tins of corned beef, Irish stew, creamed rice, as if I were living in a land of hunger. I had nostalgic letters from Edwin, too. Ibiza was not the same. The old crowd had left, the house was lonely, and Fermin still came to play squeaky music on his violin and the two old servants still pottered around prying into everything and complaining about the terrible crime he was committing by increasing the power of the light bulbs. He had applied for another scholarship, Edwin wrote. Based in Paris. He had not heard from Bernard.

Then one evening when El Vici and I were talking in his room, El Vici suddenly knelt before me, murmuring as he tried to put a ring on my finger, 'Voulez-vous me marier, moi?' The ring, he said, had belonged to his grandmother in Milano.

I was flattered, alarmed, and melancholy, for it was Bernard who still occupied my thoughts and dreams. I realized also that because I'd had the years of my twenties removed from my life I was now behaving in some ways like a woman in her early twenties who had recently left school and home and was exploring for the first time the world of men, women, sex, love. Although I did not accept El Vici's ring, I did not reject him. Was I prompted perhaps by an impulse of greed, for love at any cost? He and the family therefore concluded that we were 'engaged' and would be married in the church in Andorra. My response had been wait and see. Then, with a sense of panic, I explained that I would first need to return to London where I had 'things to see to' (as if I were arranging my life in preparation for my death), and I would then return to Andorra.

And so it happened again that during the remainder of my stay in Andorra I found myself assuming my most accustomed role, that of the passive person whose life is being planned for her while she dare not for fear or punishment or provocation, refuse. After spending so many years in hospital I was beginning to learn that in the years that followed, this role waited always for me, and much of my life would be spent trying to escape from a prison that I had entered because I was 'used to it and use is everything.'

And so I went walking with El Vici at the proper time for 'promenading'. We attended church, preparing for the late Easter Festival. Donna talked to me of what I would wear at the wedding. Introduced to me, El Vici's friends shook hands heartily and spoke friendly words. And at night curled in my featherbed nest and looking out at the snowcovered mountains behind the buildings of Les Escaldes, I thought of the day's conversation with El Vici, the plans he was making, the answers he gave to my questions, and I felt a chill alarm spreading through me at the prospect of my future life, first in Andorra, then in the south of France working in vineyards, or helping in the fur shop, perhaps living in poverty, trying to take care of *los crios*. I found myself thinking like an 'Englishwoman' going to live in the 'colonies' — 'What about the children's education, the schools?' And what of books, and reading, and my writing? What of music and art? I did not want to become one of the characters that I had seen so romantically as living figures from the paintings of the great artists. Nor did I want to repeat what I had now done several times — used poetry to put myself in human danger and to try to force a flow of love towards me. I was learning that the uses of poetry are endless but not always harmless.

El Vici went with me while I bought a return ticket to London. While he waited outside the travel agency I asked urgently, 'If I don't use the return ticket will my money be refunded?' The clerk assured me it would be.

The Easter celebration was solemnly joyful with the traditional chocolate cake in the shape of a house, the large golden wheel of cheese distributed by the priest from the food parcel from the American government, fondants and biscuits and canalones that I helped Donna make. The table was dressed with a white cloth and candles, like an altar, and even Antoine and Xavier who had been in disgrace for having thrown their Palm Sunday palms out the window into the street, sat quietly and obediently wearing their white lace collars and their best clothes. Everyone glanced lovingly at everyone else with special glances for El Vici and me, and again I felt myself under the spell of the Spanish and Italian faces with the dark glowing eyes that belonged in the paintings of the masters who 'about suffering were never wrong'. Oh why could I not be there, too, in the painting? I, in spite of my Celtic red hair, my birthplace an antipodean world where the trees like the pines of Andorra, were a serious evergreen, the colour of eternity, of sovereignty, of the forest ruling naturally with the sea, the sky, the land, the weather. My desire to belong (and how much closer may one be to belonging when one is within both the real city and the Mirror City?) increased my willingness to allow others to decide my life.

That evening I sat in my room, my typewriter balanced on my knee, typing. I heard the murmur of voices as Donna worked with Carlos and the coloured counters. I knew that El Vici was in his room, perhaps polishing his blue and white bicycle. It occurred to me suddenly that I did not know whether he could read or write . . . I was the Englishwoman again among the 'poor peasants' who could never escape while I could escape to London. I thought again of the *crios*, his and mine, loved and wanted but poor, barefooted, unable to go to school — how far did I wish to go, I wondered, in this 'broadening of experience' I had promised to the Literary Fund Committee when I applied for my grant to travel overseas?

And my writing? In a future where I was never alone, where I worked all day picking grapes, caring for children, cooking for my family . . . how could I ever be alone again, able to enter that world of imagination to explore it and try to describe it? Certainly I would be living within it in the world of the old masters but in a world where the cherubs cried and wet their nappies, where bunches of grapes moved and grew and must be picked, in millions, not merely enough to fill a bowl lit by an everlasting shaft of golden light, where dimly lit rooms with all their wonderful play of light and shadow must be lived in, cleaned and repaired and made weatherproof.

And I did not love El Vici: he simply fitted willingly into a vacant space that would soon have its natural overgrowth more suitable to the kind of life I wished to lead.

In mid-May, the very morning the road to France was re-opened, I waited with Donna, Carlos, El Vici and the children for the small mountain bus to Perpignan. There were sad farewells, much hugging and kissing and tenderness. No, I told El Vici as we kissed, I would not take his ring with me for perhaps I might lose it. The solemn wise-eyed children who perhaps knew everything (*Cain mató a su hermano Abel*) said their goodbyes. I had bought Antoine a mouth organ with blow-draw instructions; he tried to play a tune for me. I gave Donna my green cortina and the warm brown coat bought for me by my two laughing aunts, Elsie and Joy, mother's sisters. Then, with kisses again for everyone, last for El Vici, I boarded.

The snow lay in two high walls each side of the road. I sat entranced by the blue light, the unreal mountain road brooded over by the snow and the pine trees, and the way that the bus, the first vehicle on the opened road, struggled with its snowplough to clear the path for the snow was falling again. Then, arriving in Perpignan I felt as if I had emerged from a vale of darkness for suddenly the trees were light green, the earth was bathed in a soft cloud of green spring, the *right* springtime. I spent two and a half hours waiting for the train, walking in the village, sitting on the stone seat outside the cemetery, enjoying a luxury of solitude and silence, and the peace, lapped by the desolation of a small wayside station where nothing is coming or going very often, where the posters advertise other places—cities, cathedrals, oceans, other suns and skies full of bright yellow sunlight. I thought of the small railway stations on the main trunk line in the South Island of

New Zealand—Winton, Gore, Balclutha, Milton, Clinton . . . and of course walking through the cemetery recalled for me the French poems and prose that were never far from my thoughts . . . 'Qu'il était triste, le cimetière de La Semillante . . . Que je le vois encore avec sa petite muraille basse . . ., sentences that, like music, tastes, perfumes, colours, define and isolate the brooding memories, seeding the clouds, as it were, with pearls. Why do such memories unfailingly return me to my lifelong preoccupation with the sky, with alternating moments of the sun's warmth and the chill and despair of losing the sun and waiting for its return, of a life supervised, blessed and made lonely by the sky?

I boarded the train to Paris where I spent the night in the hotel by the Bastille. The next day I arrived in London to find Patrick Reilly meeting me at the station with the news that he had found a new place to stay in Clapham Common South and had he been presumptuous in renting a room for me also? The landlady, he said, wished to be called, simply, Ma.

I thanked him. What work had I to show, I wondered, for my time in Ibiza and Andorra? I quote Albert Camus for I cannot express it so well myself, 'Living is slightly the opposite of expressing. If I am to believe the great Tuscan masters, it means bearing triple witness, in silence, flames and immobility.'

Part Two

At Home in the City

London

13

In London I planned to find work and to discover by objective means whether I had ever suffered from schizophrenia. I hoped to take advantage of the offer from John Forrest to arrange an appointment for me at the Institute of Psychiatry. Although I was still inclined to cherish the distorted 'privilege' of having schizophrenia because it allied me with the great artists more readily than my attempts to produce works of art might have done, I suspected that my published writing might destroy that tenuous alliance, for I could not people, everlastingly, my novels with characters suffering from the 'Ophelia syndrome' with details drawn from my observations in hospital. I knew that the Ophelia syndrome is a poetic fiction that nevertheless usefully allows a writer to explore varieties of otherwise unspoken or unacceptable feelings, thoughts, and language.

I planned also to find an agent who would submit *Owls Do Cry* to English and American publishers while, supported by my earnings from a job, I continued writing my poems, stories, and the novel I had begun before I left New Zealand — *Uncle Pylades*.

My next preoccupation, as a result of my love affair in Ibiza, my parting from Bernard, my shortlived pregnancy, and my too ready acceptance of El Vici Mario as my future husband, was my need to gain more than an elementary knowledge of female and male anatomy and sexual practices: my ignorance even in my pretended state of 'sophisticated woman' had been appalling.

And so with Patrick Reilly's faithful and sometimes misdirected help, I began to study the Situations Vacant columns of the *South London Press* while Patrick, as before, like a conformist New Zealand conscience that had somehow travelled with me and assumed human shape, kept reminding me, 'You want a good steady job. A typist or secretary. You don't want to spend your time writing. There's no money in it. And it's not savoury.'

Obediently I went with him to the Labour Exchange in Vauxhall Road ('for the better type of worker, temp. or permanent') where my nervousness made me unable to pass the typing test without making too many mistakes.

'What about Peek Frean's then?'

Ah, Peek Frean's! Perhaps to Patrick the London equivalent of Figuretti's. I thought nostalgically of my early days in London, of Patrick's dominating kindness and his continued reference to Peek Frean's — the biscuit (digestive, dark chocolate), the biscuit factory, even the factory premises, and how I'd been haunted by the name — Peek Frean's, with the other London names Tooting Bdy, Hatfield North, Crystal Palace, High Barnet . . . these names returned with renewed power.

I murmured, knowing Patrick would reply, 'Peek Frean's.'

'Yes, Peek Frean's. You could work in the biscuit factory.'

I did not take Patrick's advice; instead, I answered an advertisement for a writer of a fashion catalogue with a mail order firm in Brixton, and after an interview with Mr Jones when I flipped through a copy of *Owls Do Cry* saying casually that I had written the book, and noting that he appeared to be impressed, I was given the job, with a copy of an old catalogue for me to study and learn the descriptions of clothing. I would work with others in a large room; writing from 'nine till five'.

It was the presence of 'others' that deterred me. I explained that I had found other work.

Next, as I was now living near the South London Hospital for Women which advertised constantly for domestic help, I applied for work as a part-time wardsmaid but my interview with the matron resulted in her advising me to apply for nursing training as she considered me to be 'good nursing material'. The older students in their late twenties and early thirties, she said, were more able to apply themselves to study and practical work: she was sure I would make an excellent nurse. I would need a medical certificate of course, but that would be no problem as I appeared to be a healthy, intelligent, capable young woman.

The ideas and the flattery lured me. I made an appointment for a medical examination, choosing a doctor with rooms nearby, and with a name that sounded absurdly fictional, and that I now reduce, for obvious reasons, to initials. Dr C. S. My medical examination was never conducted because I made the mistake of disclosing my 'mental history' whereupon Dr C. S., instantly alarmed and horrified, her horror mixed with sympathy, exclaimed that nursing was not for me. She scanned my face for 'signs' of my prolonged incarceration and what had caused it; I knew better than to say it had been a 'mistake'.

Quickly she began ushering me to the door where she paused, perhaps slightly ashamed of her haste and her ill-concealed fear. She did have a friend, she said, who wanted a maid for light domestic help, and perhaps I could work there . . . under supervision, of course. Otherwise . . . with my history . . . my condition . . .

She ushered me quickly out the door.

I remember that interview vividly: its essence is contained in the peculiarly fictional name of Dr C. S. Among my memories of London names it has a place beside Peek Frean's, Tooting Bdy, Tufnell Park . . . except that unlike these it encloses a small globule of horror.

It was not only the evil of conformity in the shape of Patrick Reilly that pursued me; my own past, too, continued to loom. How could I regain my confidence when I had never been able to tell 'my side' of the story? I knew it was time for me to find out 'the truth'.

Therefore I arranged through John Forrest an appointment with Dr Michael Berger of the Institute of Psychiatry.

In the meantime I found a job, a literary agent, and I bought an encyclopaedia of sex.

Questions

14

I became an usherette at the Regal Theatre, Streatham (women were known by the diminutive form of the word — *usherette*), where I began each day at half-past ten to prepare for the eleven o'clock session, with a break in the afternoon, and on alternate days I'd work the five o'clock or the seven o'clock session, sometimes both, finishing after eleven o'clock at night, after the routine search of the theatre for stray patrons, lost property; and newborn babies in the lavatory. I tried to enjoy the work for it was no doubt a 'broadening of experience' but it was not pleasant being in charge of a theatreful of children during the Saturday morning sessions or trying to control the teddy boys and girls in the Sunday afternoon sex-and-horror movies, or, during the intervals, playing the role of ice-maiden with my tray of orange drink, choc ices and plain ices strapped around my waist and over my shoulders and my hands in the half-dark trying to choose the correct change from my 'float', and then, later, having to pay money because I had confused the massive two shilling pieces with New Zealand halfcrowns. The staff and the audience fascinated me. In my role of 'developing writer' I 'studied' them carefully while I learned the language and ways of usherettes, how ushering in the counties was simply another job but ushering in the London suburbs was a prelude to ushering in the theatres like the Leicester Square where premieres were staged and film stars, directors, producers, made personal appearances and where an usherette at the right place and time and creating an interesting impression might find herself noticed, spoken to, perhaps on her way to Hollywood, stardom . . . the big time. This was the dream of all the young usherettes who worked with me and no doubt it was a sustaining dream for those living in the bedsitters of Streatham, Brixton, Clapham, and there was always an imagined or real example of the usherette — 'you remember her . . . only two years ago . . . who'd have thought?' — who 'made good'.

I found the work tiring and depressing: cinemas were being closed, replaced by bingo halls, and with each change of programme the managers of the Regals, ABC's, Odeons and Gaumonts, threatened with the loss of their jobs, tried to devise a more spectacular promotion. One week fake lions roared in the foyer, children took part in impossible competitions that they could never win, reminding me of the games arranged by the picture theatres in my childhood in the days of the Depression when a letter missing from a sentence to be completed with a set of letters, meant, for us, almost life or death. During the three weeks that *The Curse of Frankenstein* played, vampires, stakes, silver bullets, a model of Frankenstein, all in a mixture of horror folklore, were displayed in the foyer. And all the while the manager, a short middle aged man with an upward gaze and sandy hair looked increasingly anxious; and the usherettes dreamed of the time in Hollywood.

One free day after having chosen from the *Artists' and Writers' Yearbook* an agent, A. M. Heath, who had been the agent of e. e. cummings, and therefore I reasoned, must be willing to deal with experimental writing, that is, sacrifice money for faith in a writer, I went to Dover Street to keep an appointment with Patience Ross, of A. M. Heath. I found the office near the top floor. The general air of disorderliness surprised me — manuscripts everywhere, some piled on the floor, some on shelves, newly published books with the gloss still on their jackets displayed on stands and upon the walls, in cases, on bookshelves; photos of authors, many authors, men and women, all unknown to me.

Patience Ross, wearing black and grey with grey short hair, grey eyes, and a kindly manner, greeted me.

My first literary agent!

She reached into a large handbag crammed with books and drew out the copy of *Owls Do Cry* that she had been reading. She had been impressed by it, she said, although she did not suppose it would be of popular interest. If I agreed to allow them to be my agents they would begin submitting the book to English publishers and, through their agent in the United States, to American publishers, although I must bear in mind that publishers preferred to handle manuscripts and not books already published in another country. Did I realize, she asked, that under my contract with Pegasus Press they would be entitled to fifty percent of all my earnings from overseas? The prospect of royalties being so distant I merely smiled with an air of 'who cares?'

After the interview we left the office together in the openwork cast iron lift which Patience Ross compared to 'something out of Kafka' whereupon I, eager to appear 'like a writer' to match those daunting literary portraits on the office walls, murmured knowingly, 'Yes, Kafka . . .'

I caught the 137 bus back to Clapham South.

My next task was accomplished swiftly. I walked in to a shop in Charing Cross Road and bought a large volume, the *Encyclopaedia of Sex*, advertised in the window as having 'hundreds of diagrams and photos in colour'.

I then prepared to keep my appointment for the following week with Dr Berger.

It was my first London summer with the heat oppressively full of fumes and the pavements burning. On the day of my appointment with Dr Berger at the Maudsley Hospital, Denmark Hill, I walked from Clapham South to Clapham North along Clapham Park Road and Acre Lane, through Brixton along Coldharbour Lane to Camberwell Green, past the rows of dilapidated brick houses; everywhere was grim, dirty with an air of poverty; the voices were strange, the woman in the shops said 'luv', 'Here you are, luv,' when I bought a packet of peppermints, *Curiously Strong*; the women wore headscarves, their faces looked tired; the men were pale, of small build, like burrow animals; beggars sat on the pavement, with cap or tin beside them, waiting for money to be thrown in response to the placard propped against the wall beside them — *War Wounded, Stumps For Legs. Blind From Birth. Born This Way. A Wife and Five Children.*

I passed a shop that advertised *Horse Flesh For Human Consumption.* I read the notices in the newsagents, and the chalked menus outside the uninviting transport cafés. I arrived at a square of dried grass bordered with a few shrubs and seats and surrounded by traffic going to Peckham, Forest Hill, Central London, Clapham. I walked up the street to the outpatient department of the Maudsley Hospital where I hoped to find at last the answers to the questions I still asked myself about my 'history'. I had to know whether my own views, usually met with polite disbelief or sometimes with sceptical agreement, held any truth or were merely another instance of self-deception.

During my first interview with Dr Berger I found myself again in the familiar role of using my long stay in hospital as a means of holding his attention. I knew that such a long stay with such drastic treatments performed and planned, usually gave the conclusion that my condition had been hopeless, as well as the surmise that it could recur: I knew the effect on strangers of learning about my past. I also knew that their response could be used to accomplish my wishes. The fact that, invariably, I was forced to go to such lengths to uncover my 'secret, true' self, to find the answers to questions that, had I the confidence and serenity of being myself 'in the world' could have been asked directly, was evidence to me of a certain unhealthy self-burial. Often, after repeated earthquakes, there is little sign of what survives beneath the ruins, and if there are survivors they must first attract attention before the authorities decide to investigate and explore the remains of the city, whether it be a real or a mirror city that moves when the wind moves and is subjected to tides of ocean and sky.

Dr Berger, a tall dark pale man, with a chillingly superior glance and quellingly English voice, made another appointment to see me. Feelings of past unpleasantness and fear had been roused in me by this visit to a psychiatrist: attracting his attention and observing his serious face had reduced my store of confidence. I knew, however, that if anyone could discover the 'truth' it would be he, alone or with his colleagues.

I continued to work at the Regal Theatre. My supply of money was fast running out, and ushering became more tedious and depressing as each afternoon during the coffee break I listened to the confidences of the younger usherettes. One had been going to bed with a famous singer whom everyone thought of as perfect, you could see his kindly face on the television each evening: he had promised her a contract and, perhaps, stardom, she said. Another, learning that I hoped to be a writer, brought her collection of poems for me to read and I winced as I followed her golden moon to the month of June and looked into her lover's eyes that were blue as skies; yet perhaps I need not have winced had I thought of my own experiences.

Sometimes my father in Oamaru sent a bundle of five shilling postal notes bought on separate days and 'saved' during the currency restrictions. Miss Lincoln at Mt Maunganui also sent her bundle of five shilling postal notes.

And in the evening when Patrick Reilly and I were not working, we walked on the Common as in the days when I first came to London, and it was nearing that time of year, the blemished summer finally promising to give way in a cloud of dust and withering leaves, with the suddenly blood-filled sun stalking the city in and out through the thinning branches of the plane trees; and soon the grass on the Common would lie sparse, brown, with no hope of further growth.

I kept my second appointment with Dr Berger. I, who had been absorbing the city of London in its seasons, spoke as if I were the city, revealing myself as tired, looking towards winter. I talked of suicide. Such talk came readily to me as a shortcut to ensure action when the paths to real communication had been overgrown. I knew that talk of suicide must always be taken seriously, that it is only the uninformed who do otherwise or respond, to their later regret, with calm acceptance of the fact and the possibility of the deed. Such acceptance, an assurance that all is well, is enough to precipitate the act in a desperate person who then has no other way of making known the desperation.

It was Dr Berger's opinion that I should become a patient at the Maudsley for observation and tests. My plan had succeeded. I would now have my questions answered. Although I had many fears, I supposed that this famous Institute of Psychiatry would have few of the shortcomings of New Zealand hospitals, that it would have many doctors trained to make thorough diagnoses after learning all the facts of each case; also that, unlike in New Zealand, the 'case' would have a chance to speak, to be known at first hand. I expected much.

Dr Berger allowed me to return to my room in Clapham South where I collected a few personal belongings, and explained to Patrick who offered to store my suitcases in his room for the six weeks I'd be in hospital. In spite of my growing apprehension I did feel my action was necessary: I would at last find out 'the truth'.

The
Investigation
and the
Verdict

15

I had not known what to expect from the Maudsley. What I found impressed me and gave me cause for gratitude that I still feel. There was then an abundance of medical, nursing, domestic staff with many of the nurses from Europe, Africa, Ireland, the West Indies, and one or two from New Zealand. In the admission and observation ward the ratio was one nurse to five patients with domestic duties given to ward-maids, kitchen maids, cooks, leaving the nurses free for professional nursing. Remembering my days in Seacliff Hospital in New Zealand, in the 'back ward' where the nurses were forbidden to talk to me (I was told this later by two nurses, now retired), I was amazed to discover that here at the Maudsley it was the nurses' duty to talk to the patients, to get to know them — how else could a correct diagnosis be made? I was impressed also to find that the patients were interviewed by their doctor several times a week, at first daily, and not, as happened in New Zealand, once on admission, once on discharge, with occasional fatuous 'Hellos' between, no matter how many years the interval 'between' may have been. At the Maudsley I would have no reason to complain that decisions were made about me without anyone having taken the time and trouble to speak to me and try to know me. The Maudsley also gave numerous standard 'tests' as an aid to diagnosis (another method unheard of or at least not practised during my years in New Zealand hospitals).

There was an element of luxury, even of self-indulgence, in having a personal doctor and nurse. I was assigned a Dr Alan Miller, a young American graduate to whom I gave my personal history (omitting the large mass of the untellable) during frequent interviews. The Maudsley had already obtained from New Zealand details of my period in hospitals there, of diagnosis, treatment, prognosis.

Dr Miller was a tall burly man who was feeling the cold of the approaching English winter, and so appeared to be wearing many layers of clothes, increasing his bulk. He worried about his weight. He often ate chocolate bars during our interviews. For recreation he played the viola and was proud to correspond once a year with Pablo Casals. He had brought his wife, his children and his American Ford station wagon for his year at the Maudsley, and was lamenting that his year would be over soon. Although finding out such details about a psychiatrist was not usual, Dr Miller talked freely about himself and his feelings and opinions in contrast to the serious sober Englishmen who stared, frowned, half-smiled, and uttered only 'M-m, I see.' I was grateful to have as my doctor someone who was not afraid to acknowledge and voice the awful thought that he belonged, after all, to the human race, that there was nothing he could do about it, and pretending to be a god could never change it. And how enthusiastic Dr Miller was! 'You've never suffered from schizophrenia,' he said. 'Schizophrenia is a terrible illness.' The verdict had to be objective, however, the result of tests and observations and interviews with the team of doctors supervised by Dr Berger, with the results to be given at a meeting chaired by Sir Aubrey Lewis, then director of the hospital. Infected by Dr Miller's enthusiasm I performed and underwent tests of many kinds, mental, manual. I had my first electroencephalogram (a test which should have been given as routine years ago) and I was disconcerted when Dr Miller, always eager to communicate the results, announced that my brainwaves were 'more normal than normal', thus shattering my long-held acquaintance and kinship with Van Gogh, Hugo Wolf — inspired to blossom by the unforgettable words of the handsome charming young lecturer of years ago — 'When I think of you I think of Van

Gogh, Hugo Wolf . . . Janet you are suffering from a loneliness of the inner soul . . . '

Finally I was summoned to the interview room where the medical team sat at a long table with Sir Aubrey Lewis at the head. The team had already had its meeting and formed its conclusions, and after a few minutes' conversation with me, Sir Aubrey gave the verdict. I had never suffered from schizophrenia, he said. I should never have been admitted to a mental hospital. Any problems I now experienced were mostly a direct result of my stay in hospital.

I smiled. 'Thank you,' I said shyly, formally, as if I had won a prize.

Later, Dr Miller triumphantly repeated the verdict. I recall his expression of delight, and the way he turned bulkily in his chair because his layers of clothes appeared to hinder his movement.

'England's cold,' he said. 'I have this thick woollen underwear.' The latest fashions, short overcoats, narrowed trouser legs, added to his discomfort. Perhaps I remember so vividly Dr Miller's layers of clothes worn against the winter season because I myself had suddenly been stripped of a garment I had worn for twelve or thirteen years — my schizophrenia. I remembered how wonderingly, fearfully I had tried to pronounce the word when I first learned of the diagnosis, how I had searched for it in psychology books and medical dictionaries, and how, at first disbelievingly, then surrendering to the opinion of the 'experts', I had accepted it, how in the midst of the agony and terror of the acceptance I found the unexpected warmth, comfort, protection: how I had longed to be rid of the opinion but was unwilling to part with it, and even when I did not wear it openly I always had it by for emergency, to put on quickly, for shelter from the cruel world. And now it was gone, not destroyed by me and my constant pleading for 'the truth' allied to an unwillingness to lose so useful a protection, but banished officially by experts: I could never again turn to it for help.

The loss was great. At first, the truth seemed to be more terrifying than the lie. Schizophrenia, as a psychosis, had been an accomplishment, removing ordinary responsibility from the sufferer. I was bereaved. I was ashamed. How could I ask for help directly when there was 'nothing wrong with me'? How could I explain myself when I could no longer move cunningly but necessarily from the status of a writer to one of having schizophrenia, back and forth when the occasion *suited*? The official plunder of my self-esteem was eased by the attitude of the staff at the hospital. As Professor Lewis had said,

I did need professional help to free myself from the consequences of my long stay in hospital; in the meantime I would remain in the Maudsley while my interviews with Dr Miller continued. Once he had learned of the background of my life we talked mostly of everyday matters of the present, in a formless kind of therapy that allowed inclusion of worries of the present and of the past. We calmly dragged the lake, as it were, and watched the fireflies and the sunlight on the water, and usually let the old dead rest and the discovered dead return to their depths, while the water, momentarily clouded, cleared and became still. The one prolonged difficulty in our talks was my panic, scarcely comprehended or admitted, at the loss of my schizophrenia and my unwillingness to let it go, my urging, out of habit and a need for warmth, that maybe it was there after all, forever a part of my life?

I spent the winter cocooned in the warmth of the Maudsley. I became friends with the nurses and patients and with the kitchenmaid from Germany, *Gerda*, who enveloped everyone with kindness — 'Oh Janet, mein goodness kinder,' she'd say, smiling.

I have heard that the time when the hospital was fully staffed did pass; then, in the late nineteen fifties the staff were all highly qualified and diverse with the foreign nurses and psychiatrists bringing an extra dimension of their culture to their work. A particular example of the strength and wisdom of the management of the Maudsley was the inclusion of doctors who were themselves handicapped by disabilities, and it was often these doctors who became more easily able to communicate with their patients.

I was now preparing to leave hospital to continue with my 'own life'. It was early spring, with occasional snowstorms. Rather too directly for my comfort, Dr Berger explained that as a prelude to my 'holding down a job' he had asked Miss Baer, the librarian, to give me work in the medical library. Although it was known that I'd had two books published in New Zealand and I had an ambition to write full time, there was little evidence in the harsh publishing world of London that I would be able to make a career of writing. I had heard from Patience Ross of A. M. Heath that up to fifty publishers in the United States and in the United Kingdom had admired my *Owls Do Cry* but declined to publish it, and therefore, in some dejection, but maintaining my 'poetic' stance, I went to work in the medical library only to find, a few days later, that I was pronounced 'unsuitable'. Dr Berger then gave me the task of cataloguing medical papers in the brain museum. The brain museum! Blissfully alone, I spent many days sorting through medical journals in the company of glass display cases filled with preserved, labelled tumours and brains. I learned from studying the journals that ECT (Electric Shock or Convulsive Therapy) was commended as a means of provoking *fear* in the patient, the fear being as it were a *bonus*, and salutary — for the psychiatrist no doubt and not for the patient! Sitting there among the labelled, bottled brains I ventured to hope for the quality of strength and vigilance in psychiatrists, their continued examination and testing of their humanity without which they might become political operators infected with the endemic virus of psychiatry, politics, and some other professions — belief in the self as God.

I wrote a poem in the brain museum.

> *Dobson's tumour, nineteen fifty-five.*
> *You could not see it through his balding head*
> *or in his clouded face, or hear it speaking*
> *from his wild cries though it fanged forth speech*
> *in snakely blossoming unreason. He spent his last years hiding*
> *under a fliff of circular beetles and raging sunlight. One day*
> *a landslide of weightless rock fell, and Dobson died.*
>
> *Cremation was at Golders Green, a service held*
> *in the private chapel, solemnly his virtues extolled*
> *(the flotsam of vice as yet concealed by the full tide of grief).*
> *His widow rented a niche for his ashes in the church wall,*
> *and gave the wreath money to tumour research.*
> *But few at the ceremony ever dreamed they burned*
> *and buried less of Dobson than it seemed.*
>
> *Another lantern-slide, another joke. Nightfall.*
> *The room empties. Layers of cold cling to the varnished furniture.*
> *Once more the labelled and bottled thing is set aside*
> *on the cluttered desk among files and case histories.*
>
> *For three years now it has told how Dobson died: with my double tongue*
> *I spat at God. In formalin*
> *my prestige grows fat. I survive*
> *as Dobson's tumour, nineteen fifty-five.*

After I had worked two or three weeks in the brain museum it was decided that I should take daily leave from hospital to find somewhere to live, as I did not wish to stay in the same house as Patrick Reilly who, no doubt at my unconscious invitation, had threatened to take over my life with his behaviour as a bumptious parent. On his regular visits to me he spent the time warning me against the perils of the world, and in particular the perils of sex, for he had discovered my *Encyclopaedia of Sex* among my possessions. I was a fallen woman, he said, brandishing the book. 'No-one should know so much about their body. All those diagrams and photos!'

He opened the book at a diagram of a woman's sex organs.

'Is a woman *really* like that?' he asked, answering his question, 'I don't believe it.'

He was vehement. 'This book goes in the rubbish can tonight.'

That day, with the cooperation of Dr Miller, I told Patrick Reilly that it would be better if he no longer came to see me. I was soon to leave for America, I said, where I had friends.

Although I was disappointed that no-one suggested I continue my writing career, I hoped to find time to write, as the social worker had arranged an initial National Assistance payment until I was settled enough to 'hold down a job', as Dr Berger again expressed it. And so one wintry afternoon, not without a surge of self-pity and a feeling of isolation, I searched for living quarters. My sense of misery was increased by the thought that Dr Miller would soon be returning to the United States and I would have another doctor to talk to at the outpatient department. Along Camberwell Road I boarded a bus for Chalk Farm. I'd find a room near there, I told myself; on the map, it wasn't far from Primrose Hill. Surely a pleasant place to live! Chalk Farm was perhaps near a disused quarry on farmland with fields and *primroses* in spring.

The bus turned past Elephant and Castle, past Westminster, round Trafalgar Square, up Charing Cross Road, Tottenham Court Road, Goudge Street Station, Mornington Station, Camden, with the scene growing drearier and grimier until we came to Chalk Farm Station which, as far as I could see, was a high brick wall concealing the railway line out of Euston or Kings Cross or Paddington, with a row of dilapidated brick houses lining one side of the road. I left the bus at Chalk Farm and walked back towards Kentish Town and into Fortess Road which I read mistakenly as *Fortress* Road, and there before me was a sign, *Room to Let*.

Somewhere to live.

I rented the room. The rent was low. A basement room in an old house where every room was let as a bedsitter, it was dirty, with broken furniture, smashed window glass replaced by wire netting with the snowfilled London wind blowing through. A small anteroom by the bedsitter had a hole in the roof (the roof being the pavement at street level) to receive deliveries of coal and any other objects that might be thrown in. If I looked through the street window I could see and hear the wheels of traffic and the feet of walking people and dogs. I stayed one week only in that room. The building was cold, without heating, and when one day the electricity was cut off because the landlord had not paid the bill, I discovered, exploring, that the other tenants were poor, overcrowded, depressed by the damp, cold and dark and by the bedbugs. I spoke to a woman upstairs, at street level; her baby lay asleep in bed while the woman sat by the bed with scores of dolls' heads heaped beside her, laboriously painting the eyes in the blank faces. And now there was no light for her to work by.

As it was useless for me to try to type in a dark basement, I went into the street in search of another place and found to my delight a room advertised directly opposite, but a room in a flat, described enticingly in the advertisement. What good fortune, I thought, at once enquiring to inspect the room. I was shown to the third floor of the building, to a small room opening into a corridor with a kitchen and a bathroom at the end, and although the outlook was dreary, overlooking another of North London's brick walls, I rented the room at once, knowing that I could quickly move in from my basement room across *Fortress Road*. Perhaps as in Ibiza I misinterpreted the information: I had thought I was the sole occupant of the tiny flat, but I had moved and settled in and was rejoicing at my good fortune when I was surprised to hear one, then a second, then a third person entering and moving about the flat. Why had I not noticed that the narrow corridor held three other small rooms with my room second from the kitchen? I went to the kitchen where I found three women in various stages of preparing to cook a meal: Jane, pretty, fairhaired, a schoolteacher in her early twenties; Gloria, darkhaired, an office worker; Millicent, a librarian in an industrial firm. It was Millicent who, putting herself in charge, introduced the others and herself. I was a writer, I said. Perhaps, I said, when they asked if they could read my work, perhaps I would show them my book. I was reluctant to say the title for so much had happened since the book had been written and published that I was beginning to think of it as disintegrating, dissolving, and soon it would be nothing. Although

I knew that words and ideas and their expression may disappear, I had not realized the fragility of a published book, I had imagined that its form, presence, and multiplication might give it power and weight and permanence. And now even the title of my book was retreating from being voiced.

In my room in the new flat I again began my life as a writer, sitting each morning trying to type while I stared at the oppressive brick walls of Kentish Town. And each week I kept an appointment at the Maudsley Hospital with Dr Miller, each time realizing with growing gloom that his departure was weeks away, and when one day he introduced me to his replacement, a Dr Portion, I felt my heart sinking as I heard the crisp English accent contrasting so strangely with Dr Miller's rich cheerful voice with its accent that I had known for years, in Hollywood films. I wondered how I could possibly talk to Dr Portion.

After my discharge from hospital I renewed acquaintance with the poet Ben who introduced me to a friend, Lawrence, recently returned from living for twelve years in the United States, and as both Ben and Lawrence, like myself, had no regular work, and as they lived north of Kentish Town, they formed the habit of 'dropping in' to the flat in the early morning on their way to town, that is, to their haunts in Soho where they usually met other unemployed poets and painters and sat and talked in the *French* café where the customers always pointed with pride to the famous Ironfoot Jack, reputed to be a member, past or present, of the underworld. Often after giving Ben and Lawrence a cup of coffee, and feeling reluctant to face the Kentish Town brick wall, I'd go with them to Soho where we met an assortment of people whose ambition was to write or paint or compose, and I felt at home with them, yet saddened by their everlasting dreaming, their talking about what they hoped to produce when they knew clearly (as I knew) that while they talked and dreamed, their work stayed untouched in the loneliness of their bedsitters or their poky gas-reeking flats with share bathroom share kitchen share everything. My Kentish town wall wasn't the only formidable opponent to my working — dreaming was easier, though I did not voice my dreams. I regularly bought the weekly literary magazines and the *London Magazine* that had begun a series entitled 'Coming to London' recording the experiences of famous writers in their early days. I read eagerly of their experience with editors, agents, publishers while mentally composing my own 'Coming to London' which I would write one day and which would be full of references to poets and novelists I had met, with casual references to 'my publisher' (preferably Faber and Faber). 'Having lunch with my publisher one day . . . '

Indeed I dreamed.

When Lawrence began to look on me as his 'girl' I was agreeable but lukewarm, refusing to put myself again in danger of another pregnancy but willing to be comforted and to comfort, naked body to naked body. When Lawrence began arriving at the flat at half-past eight in the morning on too many mornings, Millicent expressed her disapproval, Jane also did not think I should entertain a man so early in the morning. Only Gloria, in the end room and apart from the others because she, too, had 'entertained men', understood, and she and I, like two sisters, had many confiding talks. During the day Lawrence and I would take the usual route to Soho followed by a 'gallery crawl' inspecting the new paintings in each gallery. This was his duty, he said. Someone must take the responsibility of looking at new paintings otherwise they hung there, with people perhaps glancing at them, but few getting to know them, and it was a dismal experience for a painter to realize that no-one bothered to look at his work. The painting suffered too, Lawrence said. Just ten or fifteen minutes was enough to restore life and hope to an abandoned painting and through it, renewed life to the painter alone in front of his easel.

Through Ben and Lawrence I met many of the 'outsiders' of Soho. Following the publication and popularity of Colin Wilson's *The Outsider*, there was some prestige in being 'outside', quite unlike my experience in New Zealand when the prestige lay in being 'inside', although when one has the prestige of being 'outside' one is then 'inside' the 'outside' . . . I visited sleazy clubs, becoming a member for the evening to gain admission. I met prostitutes, male and female and I listened to their stories, gaping impolitely as I cherished my growing 'experience of life' and quoting to myself on many occasions, 'I sit in one of the dives on Fifty-Second Street . . . '

The direction I had set myself, however, was too clear for me to be waylaid for long. Wasn't it time I applied myself to my writing? The words of Dylan Thomas came readily to mind.

> *Oh no work of words now for three months in the bloody*
> *Belly of the rich year . . .*
> *I bitterly take to task my poverty and craft . . .*

Three months only and he was in despair! Perhaps I was not 'really' a writer? My doubts returned. Perhaps the desire to journey back and forth from that Mirror City was merely an abnormality after all? Oh why had they robbed me of my schizophrenia which had been the answer to all my misgivings about myself? Like King Lear I had gone in search of 'the truth' and I now had nothing. 'Nothing will come out of nothing.'

Dr Miller decided that I should begin seeing Dr Portion now that I had met him, and so we said a brief goodbye and good luck to each other, and I felt as if all the griefs I had ever known had surfaced within me. I felt completely alone in the world, in a grey world where for months the colour had been drained from the faces of Londoners and the face of the earth, and in such a mood I found ludicrous the idea that I would ever be able to communicate with a doctor who during our first interview, with a well-meant cheerfulness and a desire to prove perhaps his wide range of interests, talked of the coming world heavyweight championship and asked me if I thought Floyd Paterson would win. Other remarks he made were just as remote from what I felt to be the centre of concern. Knowing the ways of psychiatrists I was ready to suppose that his approach was planned, scientific . . . but my feelings were that everything he said was out of tune, prompting me to select from my repertoire the more striking examples of behaviour guaranteed to command attention, with the result that he suggested I enter a North London hospital, and so after our first interview, when Dr Miller had gone from the hospital, I left with an admission form to one of them.

How well I remember the bus ride I took the following afternoon to 'inspect' the new hospital! It was a High Barnet bus, a name that then carried romantic possibilities — High Barnet, Tooting Bec, Friern Barnet . . . The bus arrived at the outskirts of London, at a point where the green buses are suddenly numerous and the red no longer travel to and from Central London but from Outer East to Outer West, Outer South to North, as if denying the existence of the London metropolis; here, near High Barnet, there were fewer people in the streets of now semidetached and detached houses. And then, near the corner, I saw the hospital I had been directed to — tall, of grey stone, menacing, like an old workhouse or prison. A feeling of terror came over me. I must keep calm, I thought, trying to subdue my rising panic. I don't have to go there. I must remember the investigation and the verdict, and not return to believing what I have believed in the past. I shall simply return to Kentish Town, face the brick wall, and continue with my writing. Yet the desolation of having no-one to 'tell my story to' surged through me. Perhaps I should never have left New Zealand. I did not long for any special place in New Zealand. I yearned, painfully, for sight of a straggly cabbage tree in a front garden, anyone's front garden, and for sight and touch of a hillside covered with golden tussock.

Sitting in the bus, I felt as if I were a child again with memories that I had never identified and that I could only think were part of the vision of 'the light that never was on sea or land', the kind of world spoken of in the Book of Revelations, and in Thomas Traherne's *Centuries of Meditation* where 'eternity was manifest in the light of day' and 'the city seemed to stand in Eden or to be built in heaven'. My feeling of isolation began to recede then as I reminded myself that London, of all places in the world, was full of poets, that the poems appearing in the slim and fat volumes of Faber and Faber and in the periodicals and journals were written by men and women who were now walking in the streets of London, entering bookshops, buying books, or just sleeping, talking, loving, eating; living their everyday lives in London. And writing their poems.

They may not have known it but they were *company* for me, their very breath kept me warm and dispelled my grief.

Dr Cawley
and the
Luxury of
Time

16

I returned sobered and frightened from my bus ride to High Barnet. The next week I was again admitted to the Maudsley Hospital. Now, without my schizophrenia, I had only my ordinary self to use to try to explain my distress. More importantly, others, the genuine 'experts' knew that I had only my ordinary or extraordinary self with which to explain myself, and this was the first such opportunity for me since I had been an adult. The prospect was a luxury as the reality would be. I know that so many live and die without tasting this luxury. I do not know what marvel of insight—or was it a gesture of impatience?—prompted Dr Berger, the consultant, to try to help me unearth myself. And who was I to suppose that I had the special right to experience a clear vision of myself and the world? Some obstinacy, some persistence in myself pursued this right until at last with the help of a combination of circumstances, coincidence, providence, and good friends, I arrived at the point of knowing the agony of the luxury of trying to tell my story, of demanding and accepting the luxury of 'the truth'.

Dr Berger assigned me to a young recently qualified psychiatrist who had been a zoologist and mathematician and was therefore above the usual age and experience of a junior registrar. I found, however, that for the Maudsley, difference was part of the usual and the practising motto may have been, 'All care in diversity'. I think I was able to accept Dr Cawley because I was aware that his view was wider, over a range of studies and disciplines and personal experience, just as I had readily accepted Dr Miller because I knew he was interested in music and art. The qualifications of medicine and psychiatry were extensions of these men, not starting and ending points. I had felt that although Dr Portion was a qualified psychiatrist, he may have superimposed life upon psychiatry and not psychiatry upon life.

I was also pleased to discover that Dr Cawley, like myself, was interested in the Here and Now and not in theories about the past, and our talks were largely at first an accounting process, an examination of my emotional, personal, and even financial budget with a view to balancing all so that I could survive in spite of the bankruptcy imposed during my long stay in hospital, and my existence since then on unreal notions of myself, fed to me by myself and others, and now my sudden extreme poverty of being myself following the Investigation and the Verdict: the wastage of being other than myself could lead to the nothingness I had formerly experienced.

I know that Dr Cawley found me a difficult patient for I was 'against psychiatry' and I disapproved of all psychiatric gods, with perhaps more tolerance of Jung; but my interviews were not an excuse for the psychiatrist to test any theories he might have had. I was disconcerted when during our first interview Dr Cawley sat with a pen and paper and wrote or appeared to write everything I said, sometimes without looking up. At first I said little. Dr Miller at least, I thought, rebelliously, 'talked' to me. Dr Cawley, however, was 'different' from Dr Miller, and if I were to preach the importance of difference my first need was to accept it in others, and so I told myself that this was Dr Cawley's 'way'. I guessed that he might have been a shy man. Like Dr Portion and Dr Berger, he spoke with an 'English' accent that chilled me when I heard it in the distance but in his presence it could not frighten me for he was not aggressive, his manner was excessively polite, his smile kindly as if these were more a protection for himself than a gift for me. I felt that he was a clever, uncertain man whose sole triumph in our interviews was the accuracy of his recording the content. Sometimes he had a cold; he sniffed, he took out a large white handkerchief like a conjuror's aid, and blew his nose.

He wore black-rimmed spectacles, magnifying, I thought, much of what he saw; and his shoes were black, well polished. He dressed as for a day in the office.

I stayed many months in hospital, and each time it might have appeared to Dr Cawley that all my problems had been solved, I would immediately present a new emergency, either through fear of being abandoned or because there was another problem I dared not mention. With time, the marvellous luxury of time, and patience, Dr Cawley convinced me that I was myself, I was an adult, I need not explain myself to others. The 'you should' days were over, he said. *You should go here, go there, be this, be that, do this, do that — you* should *you know — it would be good for you*! Lifelong, largely because of my own makeup I had been a target for the *You should*-ers, with a long interval of *You must Or Else*: it was time to begin again.

Perhaps I had sensed a new beginning or tried to advance it because one day during the past summer I had changed my surname, recording it on the necessary document. I had been issued with a new passport.

Dr Cawley's view, supported no doubt by his assessment of our interviews of many months, was that I genuinely needed to write, that it was a way of life for me, and that the best practical help for me was to arrange a National Assistance weekly payment and for me to find accommodation near the hospital so that we might continue our talks. It was his opinion also that as I was obviously suffering from the effects of my long stay in hospital in New Zealand, I should write my story of that time to give me a clearer view of my future. In his response to this lifelong urging of others to me that I should 'get out and mix', Dr Cawley was clear: his prescription for my ideal life was that I should live alone and write while resisting, if I wished this, the demands of others to 'join in'. There had never been any question of my not being able to exist in the 'real world' unless that existence also deprived me of my 'own world', the journeys to and from Mirror City, either by the Envoy who is forever present, or by myself.

The progress of healing and preparation for my life as myself in the 'real' world was such that one day I again began to look for accommodation — near the hospital, in Camberwell. I was to receive a National Assistance payment each week. I was discharged from hospital. These arrangements were made by the team supervised always by the consultant, Dr Berger, with the social worker, and with Dr Cawley who would continue to see me each week. I now had confidence in Dr Cawley, for I had not only seen myself developing and growing in his care, I had observed his own development as an assured psychiatrist who, I felt, would always respect the human spirit before the practice, the fashions and demands of psychiatry. I was influenced also by the persistence of Dr Cawley in being 'himself' and not some 'image' of a psychiatrist: he did not patronize or pretend, and when he talked of my writing, he confessed modestly, with an old-fashioned air of a character from a Somerset Maugham story, 'I'm not a literary chap, you know.'

No longer, I hoped, dependent on my 'schizophrenia' for comfort and attention and help, but with myself as myself, I again began my writing career.

Grove Hill Road
and the
Life of
a Writer

17

For twenty-seven shillings a week I rented a large front room on the second floor in the home of Ted and Joan Morgan in Grove Hill Road, Camberwell. The Morgan's daughter, Myra, and a middle aged boarder, Tilly, slept on the third floor, while my room was next to the main bedroom, with a small kitchen (to be shared with Tilly) and a bathroom and lavatory (to be shared with all) on the same floor. My room, overlooking the street, had a large mirrored wardrobe, a dressing table, a large dining table covered with a green and white checked oilcloth that I remember affectionately as I spent most of my time writing at one end, eating at the other: two chairs, one a fat armchair with outsize padded arms and floral covering, an old stretcher bed dipping in the middle beneath a mattress full of hard unevenly distributed parcels of kapok. There was a disused fireplace and a small kerosene heater.

At first, Mrs Morgan showed alarm on discovering that she had rented her room to one of those tenants frowned on in the letting world as being 'home all day' when any reader of newspaper columns and the notices in tobacconists' windows would know that the ideal tenants then were 'business woman only . . . business couple only . . . out all day' with, often, 'away weekends' as well as the usual 'no children, pets, coloured or Irish'.

I explained that I was writing a book.

'Oh, a journalist,' Mr Morgan said with some deference.

'More of a book writer.'

'We'll say you're a journalist,' he said.

He was about forty, sleek, with a coat buttoned to show his continuing sleekness, handsome, with a small moustache and a plausible manner suited to his work as a television salesman, but reminiscent for me of my idea of a con-man. Joan, in her middle thirties, was small, dark, businesslike, the part owner with her sister of a hairdressing salon 'down the Green'. Myra, who practised the piano each afternoon in the room beneath me, and played her record player each evening in the room above me, was at the serious stage of English life known as the 'eleven-plus year', with an examination looming, followed by her 'streaming' into grammar, comprehensive or high school. Myra's parents told me that one day Myra would be a clever journalist.

'You should see her essays. The talent is there.'

Tilly, the boarder, nearing sixty, who worked assembling electrical plant at the General Electric factory, and was away to work early and home late, was another Londoner whose memories of the war had matured for harmless telling. She too had come home one day to find her street, her home, her family destroyed by a flying bomb, a 'buzz bomb'. She talked often, too, of her 'post-war credits' and how their payment had been delayed by the government. 'If I'd had my post-war credits,' she'd say as she stood in the kitchen stirring her scrambled egg or her collard greens, 'life would have been different for me.' The government had failed her: she was bitter, and wary of being betrayed, and when her doctor suggested removing one of her toes to alleviate her arthritis, she saw the betrayal as extending to her own body.

Tilly was a clever dressmaker. Her whirring machine made Myra's clothes, and sewed for me a woollen skirt. 'You need it, in the English winter.'

The Morgans were naturally curious about my income. At first I did not disclose that I received three pounds seventeen and six a week from a book of National Assistance cheques to be renewed or cancelled after six months when a National Assistance inspector would call for an interview, first sending a window envelope through the

117

post with the advice, *An Officer of the Department will call*, giving the time and date. *Please be at home to receive him.* As the mail for the house was delivered early in the morning through the letterbox in the front door, on days when I expected a letter from the National Assistance Board, I, trying to preserve my secret, contrived to be first to pick up the mail. One morning I was too late. Mrs Morgan picked up the mail. I saw her glancing at the easily identifiable window envelope where some of the printing of the notice could be read through the ample window. 'It's for me,' I said, bursting into tears. 'I'm on National Assistance.'

My secret was out.

To my surprise, Mrs Morgan smiled sadly.

'I suppose you know my secret by now.'

'No,' I said truthfully.

'It's Ted—Mr Morgan. He's an alcoholic. He falls in the door most nights of the week when he's been drinking.'

She too burst into tears, and together we went to her small sitting room where she made a cup of tea and we sat talking with the intimacy that follows a newly shared secret. She explained that Ted didn't keep jobs for long, but he'd been good lately with two months working as a salesman and repairman at the television shop in Peckham Rye. (Peckham Rye. Goose Green. Dulwich. Camberwell Green.)

Later, Mrs Morgan ('I'm Joan. Call me Joan.' 'Call me Janet.') showed me the small back garden where I could hang my washing. ('I wouldn't ask anyone to use it.') She also introduced me to the grey tomcat, and as I was returning upstairs she gave me a privileged glimpse into the front sitting room with its polished piano. 'Myra has a future at the piano. And I've told you about her essays, haven't I?'

'Yes.'

We did not speak again of our broken secrets. Instead we sealed them with a new formality until it might again be necessary to break them and inspect the contents and sweep away more tears in a process similar to a periodical airing and restoring of bed linen that lay too long against our skin.

And when late one evening the door bell rang and I answered it and Ted Morgan fell through the door at my feet, Joan appeared, and not acknowledging my presence, she helped Ted to his feet and guided him into the back sitting room while I returned upstairs.

With my novel, *Uncle Pylades*, now abandoned, although the theme remains after many years, waiting, I began to write the story of my experiences in hospitals in New Zealand, recording faithfully every happening and the patients and the staff I had known, but borrowing from what I had observed among the patients to build a more credibly 'mad' central character, Istina Mavet, the narrator. Also planning a subdued rather than a sensational record, I omitted much, aiming more for credibility than a challenge to me by those who might disbelieve my record.

The book was written quickly. I kept to the routine I began when I was living in Frank Sargeson's hut in Takapuna. I also continued the method I had adopted of buying a new school exercise book, carefully writing my name in the space provided on the cover, with the word 'Novel' in a juvenile, laborious hand beside the *subject*, then ruling various columns to record timetable, progress, with spaces for *Excuses*, now called *Wasted Days* as I did not need to identify the known excuses to myself. I had already made, in my mind, an entire book from which I chose chapter headings to remind me of the whole. There was more enthusiasm than usual in my working: each week had an impartial observer in Dr Cawley to talk to and complain to and tell of my progress. Also I had news from Patience Ross, the literary agent, that an American publisher, George Braziller, with a new small firm, had decided to publish *Owls Do Cry*, while in England, W. H. Allen had shown interest and would most likely publish. As I had 'signed away' to Pegasus Press in New Zealand most of the rights of the book, the contracts would be the affair of Pegasus and not myself.

Now that I was again writing, I was sensitively aware of interruptions and each Wednesday morning when a woman came to clean the Morgan's house, I, with much complaining to myself, would take my exercise book and pen and walk or bus to Dulwich Library where I wrote, watched over by the bust of Robert Browning. My morning's work at Dulwich meant that I saved a morning's kerosene for my heater—kerosene here known as 'paraffin' and sold either as 'pink' paraffin or by a rival firm as 'blue' paraffin. One of my childish delights was to watch every second week for the 'pink paraffin man', and in discussion with shoppers at the Green or the Rye, to remain loyal to 'pink' paraffin while listening to the arguments for 'blue'.

I finished *Faces in the Water*. I showed it first to Dr Cawley whose comment was, 'It's not brilliant but it will do,' reminding me as he observed my disappointment, 'You know, I'm not a literary chap.'

I suspected that he was being modest.

He persuaded me to show the typescript to Patience Ross who liked it and when Pegasus had read it, A. M. Heath suggested I did not sign the Pegasus contract which again removed most of my rights to the book. My advance for *Owls Do Cry* was 75 pounds divided with Pegasus after a deduction of ten percent for the agent. My advance for *Faces in the Water* was 100 pounds similarly divided. George Braziller of New York gave similar advances, in dollars.

After writing *Faces in the Water* and existing through the inevitable few weeks of 'Wasted Days', I began to write *The Edge of the Alphabet*. My routine remained the same, with regular visits to Dr Cawley where I usually described the happenings of the week, and how my work was progressing. I was now awaiting the publication of *Owls Do Cry* and I knew that I was excited. I had never known a publication day in New Zealand and I wasn't sure of the English routine, although since I'd been in London I had read avidly in the newspapers of theatre first nights, art gallery private viewings, launching of books at an author's or publisher's party, with the newspapers the next day proclaiming the play, 'A hit, a palpable hit', or perhaps burying the latest works of art. Music first nights were important also, with the response to a performance in Wigmore Hall awaited eagerly by young Commonwealth musicians. The newspapers presented a world of vicarious excitement where authors, painters, sculptors, playwrights, especially if they were sons or daughters of lords or had some unusual distinguishing feature, not directly related to their work, were wined, dined, romanced, gossipped about. What if . . . ? I dreamed briefly, dismissing such dreams. I did wonder, however, how I would feel on publication day when I opened the newspaper and there were the headlines. *New Author of Fine Novel.*

My problem was, I didn't really think that *Owls Do Cry* was 'fine'!

On publication day I took the bus to Westminster, bought newspapers at the Westminster Station, took them to the lavatory in the subway, and began to read, as I thought, of my *publication*. I searched the book pages. I could find nothing. I think there was one newspaper with a small note at the foot of a 'continued' column, about a novel of poverty in New Zealand, *Owls Do Cry*. I don't think it gave an opinion.

I learned my lesson, satisfying to a person like myself who is always seeing 'sermons in stones'. Not every book published in London is reviewed, whereas in New Zealand if you were a New Zealand author your book was always reviewed. *New Zealand author writes novel*, as if you had won the Melbourne Cup or first prize in Tatts, an event that would never happen again.

Later, there were some favourable reviews of *Owls Do Cry*.

I continued with my routine of writing. If I had any practical problems Dr Cawley was always quick to help me solve them even if the solution were only a telephone call by him to the Camberwell Library to explain that I was a resident and entitled to borrow records, or recommending a dentist when I had toothache. He also became part of the routine of my work and when a typescript was finished he always allowed me to borrow a 'punch' from the hospital office to make holes for threading tape through the pages. One might ask, 'Surely it's a waste of precious time for a psychiatrist now a senior registrar to bother about minor details like lending office equipment to his patient or making it possible for her to borrow records from a library?' My biased answer would be that nothing is unimportant unless the person seeking help admits and believes it is so. I know that at my age then, in my early thirties, most women would have the help of a mate, husband, companion. I know also that there are no 'most women' and not to be one, through disinclination or disability even is not to be a personal failure: the failure lies in the expectations of others.

In the afternoon, in winter and summer, I'd go to the local cinema and sit in the warm dark planning my next day's work and watching the one-and-sixpenny double feature B movies usually made by ABC (Associated British Cinemas), black-and-white films full of murders, with opening and closing of squeaking doors, and with the camera moving cautiously around apparently empty rooms until it stayed focussed on the shocking sight behind the sofa or 'slumped' over a desk! The popular advertisement on the time was that ending 'You're never alone with a Strand' with the man in the raincoat walking the wet deserted street. Cadburys also filled the screen with their multicoloured chocolate wrappers. At half-past four I'd leave the cinema, noticing as the lights came on that many others in the audience had discovered a place to keep warm and to hide on a dreary afternoon — poor Londoners, middle aged men alone, young women with babies who cried and cried until the audience began to murmur and the usher to shine a torch on the offender; West Indian immigrants, men and women; most were alone and, suddenly illuminated, they looked like plants set the required distance from one another in some unkempt allotment by the railway line. I was such an avid cinemagoer that I travelled to all the outer suburbs seeing all the films that were shown, and each afternoon coming out into an unfamiliar place — King's Cross, Holloway, Shepherd's Bush, Tooting (the Classic cinema), Balham — where I'd venture before taking the bus home to Grove Hill Road where I'd be faced again with my writing. On many afternoons also I went to the art galleries, the Portrait Gallery, the Museum of Musical Instruments, the Victoria and Albert Museum, the Museum of Natural History where like a character in one of my stories, I used to sit for hours among the life-size reconstructions of the extinct mammoths, looking up at them, wondering about them and their world, imagining their lives.

Lately as I worked I began to hear bursts of loud music as Ted Morgan repaired radio and television sets he had brought home. When he discovered that I'd not seen much television he insisted on putting a set in my room and showing me how to work it, and sometimes in the evening I'd watch the programmes. Although the set was black and white, the people always appeared elongated, snowed upon and coloured maroon, yet I continued to watch, thinking that this was normal television, until the images grew darker and fainter.

'How's your telly?' Ted asked one day.

'My television?' I was shy of the familiar word, 'telly', as if it were a person I'd just met.

'Yes. How's it going?'

'The picture's very dark.'

'It's your tube,' Ted said.

That evening Ted replaced the tube and when he had finished tuning the set he seized me and kissed me.

'Just a token,' he said. 'Just a token.'

He had been drinking. He stayed away from work the next day, spending the time exploring the volume of his collection of televisions, and later in the week Joan Morgan told me he'd lost his job but he'd applied for another as a telephonist on the Continental Exchange. It would mean night work, she said. And he'd be sleeping during the day.

'I know you won't mind,' Joan said, 'if I ask you not to type during the day.'

I had to say I wouldn't mind: it was their home.

Then, coinciding with Harold MacMillan's election slogan, 'You've never had it so good,' Grove Hill Road became noisy as one by one the residents could afford to buy televisions and record players. My room was now penetrated by the daytime endless flow of radio talk and music, all tuned to full volume, and during the evening, the sound of gunshots from war and cowboy films. The morning offered record players that could be heard from one end of Grove Hill Road to another, that is, from the Hostel for the Blind to the pub at the corner.

Panic came over me — what would I do? Where would I go? I tried to build myself a soundproofed booth, like a telephone box, in the middle of my room, draping blankets around screens, shifting the wardrobe between me, the typewriter and the Morgan's bedroom where Ted was now sleeping during the day, but it was little use: the noise from the street and the adjacent rooms increased, and Ted was still wakened by my typewriter.

I therefore boldly bought a record player with records of Beethoven's Ninth Symphony and Schubert songs, including 'To Music' and 'Shepherd on the Rock', and when Ted Morgan had finished his daily sleep and the television and radio and record player sounds rose to full volume, I'd add my chosen music to the din while I typed. To add variety to my listening, I borrowed records from the Camberwell Library. In my struggle to get my writing done I realized the obvious fact that the only certainty about writing and trying to be a writer is that it has to be done, not dreamed of or planned and never written, or talked about (the ego eventually falls apart like a soaked sponge), but simply written: it's a dreary awful fact that writing is like any other work with the marvellous exception of the presence of the Mirror City and the constant journeys either of oneself or of the Envoy from Mirror City.

During this time *Faces in the Water* was published and I finished writing *The Edge of the Alphabet*. Again, I bought newspapers to discover what 'they' were saying about *Faces in the Water*, and I was startled to find my photo on the book page of the Sunday papers and relieved that I had changed my surname as I preferred to live anonymously in Grove Hill Road. I was amused by the *Manchester Guardian's* comment, 'Surely the use of the first person was a mistake. A woman who has been what this woman has been would never be able to remember and write about it in this way.' It was assumed that the character of Istina Mavet was a portrait of myself.

Faces in the Water was a success with reviewers and sold more copies than *Owls Do Cry*. There were foreign translations with advances less commission divided equally between myself and Pegasus Press in New Zealand, but for *The Edge of the Alphabet* the agents at last persuaded

123

me to sign separate contracts with each publisher. *The Edge of the Alphabet* before publication was among those from which 'Book of the Month' was chosen and therefore, published, was entitled to wear a gaudy yellow sash. The sudden attention to my work (not personally as the agent protected me, the supposed character of *Faces in the Water*) brought new lessons for me. When the agent and publisher received the typescript of *The Edge of the Alphabet*, the agents suggested I omit one chapter, the publishers that I enlarge the same chapter; there were other conflicting suggestions some of which I diffidently tried to follow. When the book was published, some reviews said of the now diminished chapter, 'It could have been longer,' while others praised parts criticized adversely by the agent and publisher but which I had not changed, while yet others criticized parts that had been praised. This confusing experience reminded me of what I already knew, and strengthened my resolution never to forget that a writer must stand on the rock of her self and her judgment or be swept away by the tide or sink in the quaking earth: there must be an inviolate place where the choices and decisions, however imperfect, are the writer's own, where the decision must be as individual and solitary as birth or death. What was the use of my having survived as a person if I could not maintain my own judgment? Only then could I have the confidence to try to shape a novel or story or poem the way I desired and needed it to be, with both the imperfections and the felicities bearing my own signature.

Another lesson was as personal: reading praise of me and my writing, I could feel within myself an inflation of self-esteem similar to my feelings as a child when I won school prizes or had poems published in the newspapers, and I thought as I walked along Thames Street, Oamaru, North Otago, New Zealand, the South Pacific, the Earth, the World, the Universe, 'Everyone everywhere will know how clever I am!'

Now as I walked along Charing Cross Road I thought to myself, I wonder if these people know it is I whose photo was in the paper today, it is my writing they were praising, my book described in headlines? I'd glance at the literary types in Charing Cross Road and I'd think, 'If only they knew! I know I don't dine in fancy restaurants nor am I mentioned in the "About Town" notes of the *Evening News* and the *Evening Standard* ("promising novelist seen . . . etc"), but I'm in London, I'm here, I'm secret, and I'm in the reviews and some have compared me to Virginia Woolf!'

This self-inflation lasted until, reading the inevitable adverse criticism that hurt, that seemed not to 'understand' what I had written, that seemed 'unfair', and that sometimes described me as 'a woman who had been insane', I experienced the anguish of wondering who I thought I was that I could aspire to be a writer: I, with little talent, few words. I knew I had feelings and I could see inside people without having learned about them, but these were too few qualifications: I should never have begun writing.

Once *Owls Do Cry*, *Faces in the Water*, *The Edge of the Alphabet* were published I'd had enough experience of opposing reactions to make a deliberate effort to smooth my feelings about all reviews, to allow myself to believe neither the praise nor the adverse criticism, become neither overjoyed nor depressed, and if possible not to read reviews unless it was obvious that the writers had read the book and not just the blurb and a few biographical notes (not provided by me) that referred to 'insanity', and who, understanding or not understanding the book, made intelligent comments about it.

These early lessons remained with me and helped to simplify the complex mechanism of publication where the author is in danger of being trapped and even disabled.

During the snowbound quiet of the London winter I wrote two volumes of stories from which the *New Yorker* and other magazines that I learned were known as 'glossies' chose stories. When my cheque arrived from the *New Yorker* I was amazed and guilty that what had seemed an enjoyable exercise had been rewarded with so much money. I now had over six hundred pounds in my bank account – the magic number for those on National Assistance; soon, with fragments of advances being paid, I knew I would no longer be eligible. I planned to try to move to a quieter room.

Friends
in
London

18

One day I had a letter from John Forrest whom I'd not seen for nearly twenty years although we had corresponded from time to time and it was he who had arranged my initial appointment with Dr Berger at the Maudsley. He was now passing through London, he said, and he wondered if he could say hello.

He arrived one afternoon at Grove Hill Road bringing the gift of a Mexican bracelet that, in the continuing war of some jewellery with my body, would not fit on my large wrist. Bracelets always broke, necklaces were too small, brooches came apart, earrings unclasped or were too tight.

'Never mind,' I said. 'I'll fit it later.'

Our mutual apprehension melted. We talked of ordinary matters, his work and my work. We exchanged copies of books we had written. And later we dined at the restaurant on the South Bank overlooking the Thames. We might have been on an English pier in winter. There were few patrons, an icy wind blew from the Thames, the chairs and tables had been quickly overlaid by rust in a world where the effective substances are still blood and salt and water. The next day John Forrest flew home to America knowing we were now in a level state of uncomplicated friendship and would stay there. He was still perhaps unaware of many facts of my life and of the influence of his words spoken twenty years earlier, 'When I think of you I think of Van Gogh . . .'

Another friend, more recent, also influenced my life: the National Assistance man who, I felt, decided my very existence. Even in writing my books I planned each one to be written within six months because my supply of cheques lasted six months before the dreaded notice came in its window envelope, 'An Officer of the Department will call . . .'

I knew I'd not be able to work that day. I grew apprehensive. Would I be granted my six-monthly lease of life? I'd had the small advance from my books, and the postal notes for five shillings each, sent by my father, and now almost six hundred pounds in the bank. Not ever being sure if I would be allowed to keep my typewriter, and fearful at first that the National Assistance man would seize it, I used to hide it in the wardrobe with my reams of paper.

When I first met the National Assistance man, I was surprised and saddened by his appearance. He was tall, thin, with a pale face that made him seem ill. His clothing, his shoes, his briefcase were shabby and he himself might have been an applicant for National Assistance. I discounted the thought that the Department arranged his appearance to make his clients feel at home with him! Yet if he had been dressed like a stockbroker he might not have been received so warmly by those he had set out to 'inspect'. There was nothing officious about him; he was apologetic, mournful, and efficient.

Declining my offer of a cup of tea and a digestive biscuit he smiled gently, 'I've just had morning tea next door — the top floor where the Polish family live, and then the Italians on the ground floor gave me a feast. I think I must have clients in almost every house in Grove Hill Road.'

He spoke with pleasure and some pride.

When he had finished examining my bankbook, he glanced across the room while I waited in suspense as he looked again at the television. I said hastily, 'My landlord, Mr Morgan, used to work in a television shop. It belongs to him.'

The National Assistance man smiled.

'Do you watch "Coronation Street" and "Dixon of Dock Green"? And "Emergency Ward Ten"?'

'Sometimes. I like watching the new performers. Russ Conway.'

'Oh yes, Russ Conway. My children watch it too much, I think. I've two boys at High School. Comprehensive.'

I knew that in the English world he was immediately 'placed', for schools as well as accents placed people here.

He shuffled his papers into his briefcase, buckled it shut, and walked towards the door.

'I'll see you in another six months,' he said gently.

When he had gone, I put my typewriter on its mat on the table, and the paper beside it, ready. Then I went out for a walk to breathe the air and rejoice that I was safe for another six months; and in two or three days when my book of cheques came through the mail I'd buy a bun covered with coconut icing, split it open, butter it and eat it. I had six months to write, until the next window letter came — 'An Officer of the Department will call . . . '

When *Faces in the Water* was published, I gave a copy to the National Assistance man, writing simply, 'To the National Assistance Man with thanks . . . '

John Forrest, the National Assistance man . . . and Patrick Reilly. One day when I was boarding a bus I met Patrick Reilly who was as surprised as I at our meeting.

'I thought you were in America,' he said.

'Oh?' I'd forgotten the lie I told to get rid of him.

'I went to America too,' he said.

He then described how, shortly after he thought I had arrived in America he had seen an advertisement for a salesman in Illinois, based in Chicago, how he had applied for the job, had been accepted, and had spent the winter trying to avoid burial in snowdrifts. He had learned that the company always placed tantalising advertisements in other countries because salesmen in the United States avoided travelling through Illinois in winter. He had thought it would be exciting, and the pay was high, Patrick said. He had looked up Illinois on the map. The gateway to the West. Money, a car, accommodation . . .

'Well,' I said. 'I didn't go to America. I changed my mind.'

'Where are you living?'

I told him. He frowned sternly when I said I was living on National Assistance.

'That won't do,' he said. He was working in the stationery store at Selfridges. He could visit me in the weekends, he said. And so we drifted together again.

The next weekend was to be the first of many when I, trying to make my National Assistance payment last, used to look out of the window to see Patrick, faithful Patrick, still with his jaunty walk and his bumptious air, coming down the road past the hostel for the blind, past the house next door where the Italian and Polish family lived, to the Morgans; and always he'd be carrying his Woolworths paper bag with the string handle: packed with food. I felt like a child at Christmas as he set the bottles and jars and packets on the table.

'I thought you might like this,' he'd say. 'Or this.'

There was always an assortment of Peek Frean's biscuits, Irish bacon and butter, a Hovis loaf, tinned creamed rice or white grapes: Patrick's channel of communication was food. Usually he brought enough to supplement my ordinary supply for a week. He brought me notebooks, too, as my father had done when I was a child, from his workplace. His resemblance to my father, particularly when his lips pursed with disapproval, was uncanny and caused me to wonder about myself and my life. Dr Miller had said frankly that he thought my father was a bully; he had a similar opinion of Patrick Reilly. My life had been erased, almost, by expert bullying while I played the role of victim that like any other repeated role, resists a change.

Patrick became the provider, the companion. He gave no sign of wanting to touch or kiss me; if he accidentally touched me he said, 'Excuse me, I'm sorry.' I depended on him yet I found him repugnant; I felt no sexual desire for him. I liked him best when he talked of the leprechauns and the Irish language, and we shared a love of weather, of sky and sea and green, and as we had done in my early days in London, we walked in Ruskin Park or on Clapham Common where he now had a single council flat on the ground floor.

And when Patrick learned that I'd never been to a circus and there was a circus booked to appear on Clapham Common, he bought tickets for us, but on the morning of the expected performance he appeared with the news that the circus had been rained out in one of those local storms that strike separate suburbs of London. The circus had gone north, Patrick said.

We walked on the Common where the tents and caravans had been. The ground was like a Southland cowbyre in winter, churned with mud and hoofmarks. And it was not Patrick but I with my didactic leanings who suggested that perhaps I had been 'meant' not to see a circus.

Patrick and I had a memorable Whitsunday during those Grove

Hill Road days. He arrived for his usual Saturday visit. 'Next week's Whit,' he said while I listened with delight at the abbreviation — *Whit*. 'What are you doing for Whit?'

'Nothing,' I said.

'Oh you can't be alone for Whit.'

He was cooking a turkey, he said, and I was to come to his flat and share the Whitsunday dinner.

The next Sunday I arrived at one of those tall apartment buildings that replaced the bombed houses and were named after various Englishmen — Tennyson House, Milton House . . . Patrick's flat was tiny like the corner of a cardboard box of the kind my sisters and I used to divide into a house for our kewpie dolls.

A large cooked turkey crouched on a plate in the middle of the table beside a dish of tinned peaches, a jug of whipped cream, chocolate digestive biscuits unwrapped and parted from one another in a semi-circle on a plate. There were ABC scones freshly buttered with Irish butter; and two Lyons individual fruit pies to eat with the peaches.

The meal was the thing, as if Patrick were a marksman arrowing in on it. I followed his example We started on the turkey and when dinner was over much of the turkey and the dessert remained, and when I left for Camberwell Patrick walked me to the bus stop, inviting me to the church nearby where we sat subdued by turkey and peaches and individual fruit pies before the crucifix. I admired Patrick for his fierce protectiveness towards *his* church, and the fervent way he tried to persuade me to belong, to give up all evil. We could go to the priest for instruction, he said.

'But I believe in divorce,' I said.

We argued over divorce. I was full of platitudes in many of my arguments as if I were again an ignorant student trying to discourse on 'free love', determinedly opposing all beliefs of the 'older' generation, for, in my view, Patrick was an older generation because he came from an older civilization where it was not so easy to be rid of embedded belief.

The next weekend, as he unpacked his carry bag of food and I asked how he had spent the rest of Whitsunday, he looked ashamed.

'I ate the whole turkey. The whole turkey. As soon as I got home I started on it and ate and ate.'

He looked uncomfortably surprised by his actions. Gluttony was a sin and sins were serious.

'To tell you the truth,' he said, 'there was nothing else to do.'

His words were an admission of such awful emptiness that I felt helpless, imagining him stifling time with a cooked turkey. The dreariness depressed me. I knew that London was full of people like Patrick. Didn't I, too, spend all afternoon in the cinema, to get warm, certainly, but also to *mark* time, to disguise time, *mask* it, when I needed to escape from my work when it frightened me; I, too, paying my admission fee in daylight, emerging in darkness, feeling robbed of the hours between but grateful for their passing, as if Time and I were partners. And later, home at Grove Hill Road, regretting the vanished hours, I'd think, 'I can't believe I deliberately banished so much time.'

Poor Patrick! He may not have been happy with his consuming almost a whole turkey, but I, in my turn was unhappy and guilty over using him as a provider, continuing to accept his gifts while feeling irritation and dislike for him. He thought always of what he might give me, his giving taking the form of *goods*. We'd be walking along the street and he'd say suddenly, peering into a shop window, 'Look, that's what you want. That's what I can give you.'

Or he'd stop and gasp as an idea came to him, 'I know what I can give you. I know what you would like.'

Books, a fountain pen, underwear . . .

I accepted all with a voiced gratitude but with a feeling of dislike both for him and myself that we were apparently so unskilled or inadequate that we relied for our human trading upon the currency of a world of commerce. Perhaps it was enough. Men and women have always used the materials around them to supplement, enhance or replace or transform the material within themselves. My laborious journeys to and from Mirror City were another instance of the politics of use.

It was Patrick's renewed attempt to select my friends that finally parted us. I had kept in touch with the poet and painter of North London. They too had been marking time with their desperate signatures. Ben who had visited me regularly in hospital bringing the comfort of books, ideas, news about the world of Soho and Charing Cross Road, had now embraced a 'new' psychology which was old to me as I had studied it nearly twenty years earlier. Uninhibited expression was the thing, he said, although he knew and I knew that this was only another way of avoiding the responsibility of creating order, and when I questioned him on this he assured me that order

131

came naturally from chaos. I was more sceptical. What if it remained chaos and you were caught in chaos and *Time* passed?

Ben smiled ruefully. 'Oh, time,' he said, adding thoughtfully, 'Aye. Aye,' as if perhaps because he had been to Scotland and had met Hugh McDiarmid, then Hugh McDiarmid, with Time obviously in his control, would take care of time for Ben, too. 'The thing is to be free, to do as you wish when you wish.'

I admired Ben's persistence. In a café, he'd suddenly get to his feet and begin whirling his arms like a windmill and calling out words that came at random, then he'd meow like a cat, or perhaps sing the line of a song, or begin hopping. Then he'd sit down, saying, in an aside, 'Free expression.'

When Patrick arrived at Grove Hill Road one Saturday afternoon to find Ben there, and I introduced them, and later Patrick said, 'Poets and artists are no good. Have nothing to do with them,' I felt like a clinging insect that had glued itself to the wrong plant in the wrong garden in the wrong world. Wrong for the insect, the plant, the garden and the world.

I shook myself free of Patrick.

I retreated again into my own habitat, looking out at all worlds. Working day by day, and still hoping that I might be able to find a quieter room, I finished *Scented Gardens for the Blind*. Dr Cawley, advancing in his profession, was transferring to a post in Birmingham; he was not lost to me, however, for it was arranged that he retain a post at the Maudsley where he would see me during his frequent visits to London.

And while I was absorbing this change I answered an advertisement to rent a cottage in Suffolk at a reduced rental in return for looking after the property and a dog. I had a letter from my London publisher ('my London publisher'!) arranging a meeting, and a letter from Patrick Reilly to say that London was too evil therefore he was returning to Ireland. I never saw him again.

Meeting
the
Publisher

19

When my landlady knew that I was to have my first meeting with
my publisher, she made an appointment for me at her hairdressing
salon 'down the Green'.

'I've never said anything to you before, but you must do something
about your hair. We could wetten it and straighten it.'

The old echoes. I smiled to myself. Well, I said, it was time I had
a haircut and the publisher had asked for a photo.

Meekly I fell into the preparations for the occasion. I even took
the bus to the West End where browsing in Marks and Spencer's for
a dress, I bought a patterned green and white and black jersey silk,
shortsleeved with a tie belt, and as soon as I arrived home and paraded
in front of the wardrobe mirror with my newly washed, cut and
flattened hair that gave me the appearance of having had the top of
my head sliced off, I knew that I had chosen the ugliest dress I had
ever worn. Seen in daylight, the colours were dreary, the pattern busily
confused. I stared at the stranger in the wardrobe mirror and saw
myself as I had been years ago—trapped, miserably, obedient, and
I was relieved that writing a book did not entail a visit to a 'writing

salon' where one's words were cleaned and snipped by someone trained for the purpose. I tried to roughen my hair to its old mop and halo of curls but it was useless.

I set out to the Strand and the publisher W. H. Allen in Essex Street. I sat in the bus enjoying the familiar route — around the corner past the world headquarters of the Salvation Army with its statue of Gore Booth, opposite the Denmark Hill railway station; I remembered the train crash in the first November smog after I had returned to London — my first experience of local drama in the focus of every London newspaper, the radio and television news with their lists of the dead and injured, the names of the stations — Forest Hill, Dulwich, the pictures of the fleet of ambulances ferrying to and from the South London hospitals, the comparison to the blitz, all in the first choking swirling smog of winter, the accepted signal then of the season's arrival and for the increasing daily tally of the deaths of the frail old and the cold poor.

Now down past the Institute of Psychiatry, the Maudsley Hospital, King's College Hospital, to the 'Green' with its Odeon painted an ugly dog-mess brown, past the new council flats, the dilapidated shops, the surge of the East Street market and cluttered pavements, past the Elephant, the Eye Hospital, the Old Vic, Waterloo Station, Waterloo Bridge to the Strand. A number 68 bus, its destination still, mockingly, *Chalk Farm*.

I had my photo taken in a PolyFoto studio at Charing Cross. Then I walked back towards Essex Street, loitering as I was too early, by looking in shop windows. And then I had turned the corner from the Strand and was in Essex Street, standing in front of W. H. Allen. Having observed in my early London days the various publishing houses of London when Ben and Lawrence and I used to walk up and down outside the publishers in Great Russell Street, trying to imagine the activity within and wondering, would we ever?, I knew that publishing houses were not as I had supposed they would be — palaces equal in majesty to the influence of their complete book list — and were more often like any other place of business, perhaps seedier, more unkempt. My disappointment at this discovery was tempered by knowing that within the buildings, books outnumbered people and maintained power and influence, ruling from their floor-to-ceiling shelves while the stack of untested manuscripts sat confidently waiting their turn.

Mark Goulden's office was suitably booklined with windows facing

134

the street; a thick carpet, and a large desk where Mark Goulden sat while I sat in the deep easy chair and thought, so this is my English publisher. I thought he looked like a bookie or a 'spiv', a small grey-haired wiry man with a 'weathered' face. A gambler-publisher. His voice was rich, musical, his eyes quick, lively. He said that although my books had excellent reviews, they did not sell: he was hoping that some day I would write a 'bestseller'.

He then began to reminisce while I listened fascinated as he referred to the current controversy over who had 'discovered' Dylan Thomas, and the recent published statement by Edith Sitwell supporting Mark Goulden's claim that *he* had discovered Dylan Thomas when, as an editor of a small poetry magazine, he received a number of poems which led him to want to meet the author who was then invited to London.

Mr Goulden waved his arm in the direction of the Strand.

'We put him up at the Strand Palace,' he said.

Yes, he repeated, he had discovered Dylan Thomas.

He then described other authors while I listened enthralled by his charm and his power as a raconteur. He was evidently a joyful man, delighting in himself and others.

'Where are you living?' he asked, adding that he didn't care for his authors living in a waste land like Camberwell.

'I think I'm going to stay in a cottage in Suffolk,' I said.

'You don't want to bury yourself in the country, either . . . We could give you an apartment in London while you write your new book.' Shyness overcame me. I was also wary of apartments that I couldn't afford, and he hadn't said he would pay.

'I'll see,' I said.

'Remember, if you get tired of living in the country and want to come to London, we can give you an apartment.'

'Yes.'

What did 'give' mean? Was it used in its general sense?

Mark Goulden walked to the window and looked down at Essex Street.

'When Wanda Lyons comes here she comes in a Rolls Royce. You're a better writer than Wanda Lyons. You should have diamonds and furs, and when you come to see me again I want you to be able to arrive in a Rolls Royce.'

As I was leaving he gave me two novels to read.

'These have been bestsellers,' he said.

He had painted a picture of such impossible glory for me that I felt afraid. I walked along the Strand to Charing Cross Station where I went to the ladies lavatory and cried.

When later I described to Patience Ross my meeting with Mark Goulden, I was surprised that her voice held a note of awe.

'You've met Mark Goulden?'

'Haven't you met him?'

'Oh no. Agents don't usually meet the publishers.'

I had not understood that in the United Kingdom literary agents were looked on by the publishers as intruders rather than allies.

'What do you think of him?' Patience Ross asked.

'Oh he's a wonderful man,' I said. 'A wonderful storyteller.'

'Yes, I've heard that about him.'

Was I mistaken in detecting envy in her voice? I knew that Patience Ross, now nearing retirement, had a high reputation for integrity, judgment, literacy, literary knowledge, and I felt sad that another instance of 'class' in London had denied the publisher the rewards of meeting her.

When I returned to Grove Hill Road, I found that Joan Morgan, anticipating my probable move to the country, had already found a new tenant for my room. She would increase the rent also, she said. And before I left would I do a favour for the Morgans? Myra who had passed her eleven-plus and was applying for a place at the Mary Datchelor Grammar School specializing in music, needed a reference from outside her family. Would I kindly sign a reference for her?

'Of course.'

I had watched Myra growing. I had written verses about her and her family. I had travelled with Myra to parts of London during the music competitions where I heard her play her 'piece', followed by the inevitable prodigy, the small boy (dressed like young Mozart) who had to be lifted on a cushion and whose tiny fingers played a Mozart sonata . . .

Ted Morgan brought the reference for me to sign.

I wrote my name, and in the space, *Occupation*, I wrote, *Author*. Ted Morgan produced another form.

'Would you mind filling it in again?' he said. 'This time say you're a journalist.'

Dutifully I wrote, 'Journalist'.

Ted Morgan beamed.

'Authors are thought to be unreliable,' he said. 'But when they know we've had a *journalist* staying in the house . . . '

That evening I had a phone call from the owners of the cottage in Suffolk. Would I go to their place in *World's End* for an interview?

A Cottage
in the
Country

20

World's End? I caught the bus to Chelsea, along King's Road past
the gasworks to the house where the owners of the cottage lived, and
as they showed me into the cosy downstairs sitting room and prepared
to serve afternoon tea, they told me, echoing each other, how they
had bought and renovated the Suffolk cottage and were now renovating
their home here in King's Road. They were a Miss Wilson and a Miss
Collins who asked to be addressed as *Will* and *Coll*, and they worked
as receptionists in the Moorfields Eye Hospital. Coll who was English,
perhaps in her late thirties or early forties, was daintily built,
darkhaired and obviously fastidious about domestic matters: her
interest was antiques, she said. Will, from Australia but an English
citizen for many years was less contained with a personality more easily
ventilated: one might compare two pine cones, one dark, shiny and
closed, the other, easily ripened, with open shutters. They were
enthusiastic about the Suffolk cottage that had now had its roof
rethatched, its furnishing replaced in keeping with the period, and
they were eager for me to know that both the cottage and the house
had been paid for by savings out of their salaries, and they themselves

had undertaken renovations, working long hours in weekends. Their problem was that they were unable to use the cottage until they retired and it needed a tenant, the right tenant to care for it all year. There was also a dog to be walked and fed. They'd had many replies to their advertisement, including a telegram from a retired Colonel, *Will accept cottage. Arriving weekend with five hounds.*

The idea of a writer living in the cottage seemed to appeal to them. They had even planned where I would work — at an old sewing machine placed directly before the picture window looking out at the rose garden, the lawn, and the ninety-foot lilac hedge.

'There's a rose garden that you'll be looking after. The ninety-foot lilac hedge also. And we'd like a vegetable garden. And there's the dog, actually a mongrel bitch, Minnie, belonging to an old woman living in a cottage down the road, but we've taken over Minnie for her.'

So I was suddenly the appointed caretaker, at a third of the normal rent, of a thatched cottage at Braiseworth, near Eye, in East Suffolk. (As I had recently finished writing *Scented Gardens for the Blind*, I felt bemused by the women's work at the eye hospital, and this postal location of the cottage, *Near Eye.*)

They explained how I should get to the cottage. They were enthusiastic pronouncing the place names in East Suffolk like incantations.

'Stowmarket is the place,' Coll said.

'Stowmarket?' I too was captured by the names.

'Stowmarket. When you have your belongings put on the train, remember they travel only as far as *Stowmarket*, and from there you hire a carrier to deliver them.'

'And remember, you're not going to Suffolk *proper*.'

'Not Suffolk *proper*?'

'No, it's *East* Suffolk. It's apart and different and quite *unspoiled*.'

Their voices were rich with the satisfaction of praising East Suffolk.

They would go to East Suffolk that weekend to prepare for my arrival in three weeks, they said, and they'd be waiting for me the weekend I arrived, to welcome me.

'And if you're coming by bus you ask for the Braiseworth turnoff and turn right down the oak lane . . . '

'Turn right down the oak lane,' I echoed as I caught the bus home to Camberwell. The words had the magic of directions given and followed in fairy tales, myths and legends.

Three weeks later I took the train from Liverpool Street Station to Ipswich where, changing to an Eastern Counties bus, I travelled to the 'turnoff at Braiseworth' and 'turned right, down the oak lane', walked down the oak lane to the cottage where Will and Coll waited to receive me and instruct me in my duties as caretaker.

They had prepared a bedroom upstairs below the sloping roof, with a dormer window and dark exposed beams and a view over the fields surrounding the cottage, and the ninety-foot lilac hedge just beginning to bud. Downstairs they had thoughtfully cleared the top of the old sewing machine and arranged a likely place for me to work where, as they said, I could gaze out of the window 'for inspiration', at the ninety-foot lilac hedge. They kept noting its length and describing how it would appear in flower, and remembering that they had both fallen in love with the cottage but when they saw the lilac hedge they knew the cottage would be their home. They'd installed hot water, with the Raeburn stove, a flush lavatory, and a bath. Coll, with her special feeling for roses, had planted the rose garden while Will had cleared the paths and repaired the front gate and searched until she found the heavy oak door to replace the too modern glass-panelled door with its frosted picture of a stag beside a mountain. East Suffolk had been the most wonderful discovery of their lives.

'Can you believe it?' they asked ecstatically as they toured the garden.

Later the next day Will and Coll drove back to London, leaving me alone with Minnie the mongrel bitch, my typewriter, the country quiet, and my plans for my next book.

I now thought of myself as living the life of a writer, for my two books of stories had been published and *Scented Gardens for the Blind* was about to be published, and during my time at Grove Hill Road I had been aware of a subtle shifting of my life into a world of fiction where I spread before me everything I saw and heard, people I met in buses, streets, railway stations, and where I lived, choosing from the displayed treasure frag-ments and mo-ments that combined to make a shape of a novel or poem or story. Nothing was without its use. I had learned to be a citizen of the Mirror City. My only qualification for continuing this autobiography is that although I have used, invented, mixed, remodelled, changed, added, subtracted from all experiences I have never written directly of my own life and feelings. Undoubtedly I have mixed myself with other characters who themselves are a product of known and unknown, real and imagined; I have created 'selves'; but I have never written of 'me'. Why? Because if I make that hazardous journey to the Mirror City where everything I have known or seen or dreamed of is bathed in the light of another world, what use is there in returning only with a mirrorful of me? Or, indeed, of others who exist very well by the ordinary light of day? The self must be the container of the treasurers of Mirror City, the Envoy as it were, and when the time comes to arrange and list those treasures for shaping into words, the self must be the worker, the bearer of the burden, the chooser, placer and polisher. And when the work is finished and the nothingness must be endured, the self may take a holiday, if only to reweave the used container that awaits the next visit to Mirror City. These are the processes of fiction. 'Putting it all down as it happens' is not fiction; there must be the journey by oneself, the changing of the light focussed upon the material, the willingness of the author herself to live within that light, that city of reflections governed by different laws, materials, currency. Writing a novel is not merely going on a shopping expedition across the border to an unreal land: it is hours and years spent in the factories, the streets, the cathedrals of the imagination, learning the unique functioning of Mirror City, its skies and space, its own planetary system, without stopping to think that one may become homeless in the world, and bankrupt, abandoned by the Envoy.

With these preoccupations I allied the more earthly duties of caretaker of the cottage in the oak lane, Braiseworth, near Eye, with my morning beginning, not as planned, in availing myself of Will's and Coll's promised inspiration, but in walking Minnie, and in performing other tasks — cleaning the cottage, preparing the vegetable garden, riding the three miles on the old bicycle to Eye for groceries and dog meat, and making a regular all-day visit to London to talk to Dr Cawley. My time was consumed. I spent spare moments gazing with admiration at my newly dug and planted garden and with horror at the nettles that grew twice as tall after I had scythed them. Nor was there time in the evening, for unfamiliar with the gas lighting, I used it seldom after trying to light the lamps and finding their mantles collapsed in my hand when I touched them. And so in the evening I took a candle upstairs and tried to read while Minnie lay on a rug near the door, her everwatchful glance divided between me and the door. She had quickly become attached to me, although I had been warned that she was savage with strangers and indeed was under a court ruling which ordered her to be destroyed should she again attack.

Tired enough by my daily routine as caretaker, I was not prepared for the exertions of the weekends when Will and Coll came to stay, determined to enjoy every minute and every delight of their cottage which they called, simply, *The Cottage*. Their first weekend was an alarming, exhausting intrusion. Certainly the terms of my tenancy were that I should care for the house, the dog, the garden, but I did not expect that on Saturday afternoon Will and Coll would set up their deckchairs in the sun while they suggested (ordered would be a more suitable word: they had met in the army) that I climb the ladder and remove all the dead lilac blossoms from the ninety-foot lilac hedge, working my way along each side. Otherwise, they said, the lilac wouldn't last, it would vanish in a few weeks, and what would they do, knowing they had wasted the precious lilac? My next task was to prune the rose bushes and to weed the garden borders ('you must keep the garden free of weeds'), and while I toiled most of the afternoon, snipping, pulling, tearing; redfaced, breathless and hot, I watched them lounging in their deckchairs as if they were passengers on a cruise ship observing the fascinating work of the crew. Now and again they gave more directions or pointed out weeds that I had missed, or a bunch of dead lilac, 'See, right on top of the hedge, up this end.' Sometimes they closed their eyes and basked; or they caught up with the news and the advertisements in Will's favourite magazine, *The Lady*.

Their abundance of plans fascinated me. But how could they find time, they asked. 'We've taken on too much with the cottage,' they admitted. They were glad to have a caretaker; in the winter they'd not be able to get to Braiseworth.

My experiences and impressions of East Suffolk, the inhabitants, the countryside, were absorbed to emerge later when I returned to New Zealand and wrote *The Adaptable Man*. And because my life had shifted, as I have described, to Mirror City, I now watch the story of myself receding also to Mirror City, for under the light of the ordinary sun and the ordinary day, the 'real' experiences hold diminishing interest for me, for these are the scraps only of the ultimate feast. The more I lived as a writer, the less interesting to outward eyes my life became, ruled by routine, and even in Braiseworth near Eye, with my writing crowded out by domestic duties of *garden, clean, walk the dog, shop*, the Mirror City stayed in my mind as the true desirable dwelling place.

On the days when I had an appointment in London I woke early, cycled two miles to the nearest railway station, Mellis, left my bike with the stationmaster, and caught the train from Norwich to London; or the bus to Ipswich and the train from Ipswich. Approaching London, I felt the excitement of coming home, the train gathering speed, the countryside left behind for the brick oceans, the dirty city, the squalid warehouses and factories of East London — ah the delight! — and Liverpool Street Station, just in time to step out to the marching tunes played over the loudspeaker and encouraging the ten o'clock city workers to a brisk pace.

Then I'd make my way to Camberwell to see Dr Cawley who'd also made a journey, from Birmingham; and we were like two who come from distant lands for a summit conference, to discuss important plans and futures. And after we'd had our talk I'd just have time perhaps to browse in Charing Cross Road or the Strand before I caught the one-thirty train to Ipswich, and the bus to Braiseworth. I'd arrive home to be welcomed by Minnie, and feeling tired and wondering why I was living in the country when it was the city that attracted me, and wondering where my writing day had gone, I'd go to bed in the twilight and watch the blossoming of the country dark and listen to the creatures outside, and hope for the sound of the nightingale. And alone in the cottage I was surprised to realize that I was afraid. For the first time in my life I was living alone in a house and I was afraid. If at any time I was in one room, who occupied the other rooms? I'd open the doors and look in. Nothing. I could have been adrift on an ice floe. Sometimes I heard the fluttering of a bird caught under the mesh that covered the thatch. How different the night was from my childhood night in Wyndham when the dark was as dark and I listened, afraid, to the night sounds, and thought:

Hark Hark the dogs do bark
the beggars are coming to town,
some in rags, some in bags,
and some in velvet gown.

But then I was surrounded by the warmth of people and I knew that in the kitchen the fire was burning, the room was lit by the lamp and the candles and the firelight, there was laughter and singing, and the baby was asleep.

In Suffolk I always welcomed morning and light. I was as eager as Minnie to go walking in the dew-wet lanes, watching the hares in the corn, seeing the wildflowers, primroses, cowslips, bluebells, blackthorn; but my heart was in London, I wanted to return there where I was happy to be alone in the crowd, surrounded and sustained by the immensity of people, of the human race, who, although it — we — had destroyed or crippled much of the natural world, including my northern hemisphere sky, could still send representatives to explore the Mirror City, and though some might be lost there and never return there were always those who struggled home to create their works of art.

And so when my publisher wrote reminding me of his offer of 'an apartment in the city' I thankfully accepted it, provided I could pay my usual rent. I knew from the nature of gifts, the contract between giver and receiver, that no gift is 'free', and so I thought it better to remove the apartment from the complex status of 'gift'.

I explained truthfully to the owners of the cottage the reason for my abrupt departure and I hoped they would understand· I would remain at the cottage for a few weeks until they found a replacement. I had been growing increasingly alarmed at the thought of spending a snowy winter alone with a dog in a dark house full of collapsed gas mantles, for even under the supervision of Will and Coll I never learned to touch the mantles and leave them unharmed, as each time I touched them they dissolved into powdery substance in my hand and I was reminded of my attempt at writing poems that behaved in the same way when I fingered them or tried to set them alight.

Will and Coll tried to be understanding about my betrayal of them, and I could see my alarm about a winter in Suffolk — East Suffolk — transferred to them as they wondered how they could lure a tenant without first offering the luxury bait of summer in the oak lane and the fields of Braiseworth near Eye; and when they warned me I'd be returning to the noise of London I did not list the corresponding noises of Suffolk — the daylong shots as the farmers tried to scare the crows from the crops, the roar of tractors and harvesters, the loudspeaker that sounded as if from a perennial fairground that I searched for and could not find. I did not describe to them the exhaustion of spending each day walking, planting, weeding, pedalling, instead of, as they and I had imagined, sitting at the old sewing machine table gazing through the picture window at the well of inspiration, the ninety-foot lilac hedge.

Their disappointment was lessened by the sight of the bountiful garden with its many varieties of vegetables and herbs. They were impressed, too, that I had dug a larger, deeper plot, presumably for further planting before winter. I did not explain that, discovering that the straight road at the end of the oak lane was originally a Roman road from Ipswich to Norwich, and having already unearthed a collection of stones that I washed to reveal pretty colours and designs and — with little effort of imagining — pictures, I had been seized by the fever of finding ancient relics, and thus each day I had extended the original garden till it grew wider and deeper and longer as I dug my pieces of flint, my imagined household gods and Anglo-Saxon jewellery . . .

For my first night in London before moving to the South Kensington apartment rented for me by my publisher, I stayed at World's End, with Will and Coll. I ate their perfectly cooked meal. I listened again to their marvelling at what they had done with a small house at World's End and a three-hundred-year-old cottage in East Suffolk, and I apologized again for cutting short my tenancy.

'Perhaps you'll put us in your book?' they said.

'I'll help with your suitcase,' Coll said as the next morning I walked to the bus stop on the way to Kensington. 'It feels as if it's full of stones.'

Half-full of English, Roman, Saxon, Danish stones, relics from another city.

An
Apartment
in the
City

21

It was a basement apartment with windows looking out over two streets, the large sitting room and kitchen facing the busier streets, the large bedroom beside the quieter 'place', with the bathroom enclosed in the hallway. The pebble garden at the back was planted with spiked shrubs of the kinds that, growing by the sea, suffer the salt spray and winds by bending their backs and heads forward away from the storm, and, growing in a city, adopt the same pose to avoid the fumes, soundwaves and odious smells, and in both cases they survive and bloom with thorn crowns and small blue and pink flowers. When the trucks passed along the back street the apartment shuddered with grindings, slammings, squealing of brakes, while outside the bedroom the traffic though quiet, was unceasing.

The apartment was luxurious for me. For the first time since I had been in London I had hot running water and a bath and bathroom and kitchen to myself. The furnishings were luxurious also, with striped Regency sofas and chairs with round bun-like seats, and dark polished chests of drawers. The double bed had sheets and blankets wide enough and long enough to tuck in and the mattress was as level as a wooden shelf and as unyielding, while some of the towels in the linen cupboard were labelled *Bath Sheets*.

At first I arranged my workplace in the bedroom only to find the room was too dark and I felt I was missing events in the sitting room, therefore I tried typing there beside the inner wall but the sounds of traffic intruded. I was also intimidated by the fine furniture. In a half-hearted way I leafed through the poems I had written during my East Suffolk days, and the book I had begun but my mind was occupied by the publication of *Scented Gardens for the Blind* and the sentence from a review that I could not ignore: 'This book is unreadable in the worst sense.' I struggled against losing my small supply of confidence. In another journal someone had described the book as 'likely a work of genius.' The two opinions, extreme yet balancing, shifted from me like alternatingly oppressive and buoyant waves, leaving me a damp survivor, jetsam of yet another flow of reviews.

In South Kensington I learned more about life in London, of the ease of living in SW7 compared to SE5, for a miracle seemed to occur in libraries, museums, shops as soon as I gave my address: I was treated with kindness, I was offered credit; and could they call me a taxi? The tendency to questioning and suspicion by the keepers of Camberwell had vanished. And when I walked along the streets of Kensington and Knightsbridge, jostled by the beautiful and the rich, I found myself remembering the dream of my Aunt Polly in Petone, New Zealand, to be 'someone'. 'I'd like to be somebody,' she'd say, reminding herself that she had relations, town clerks or mayors, lawyers or doctors, who were 'somebody'. In Kensington I too was 'somebody', but not because of my actions or works or some remarkable personal trait: I was 'somebody' because my address was South Kensington SW7. I had a luxury apartment with a bathroom, a white entry phone as well as an 'ordinary' telephone, a tradesman's entrance and a private entrance . . . I was out of step, however, with the dwellers of South Kensington. In Grove Hill Road SE5, getting up very early and starting work, I'd know a feeling of being at home as I saw the lights in the houses and imagined the hasty breakfasts, and watched the workers hurrying through the half-dark to catch their buses, and, later, the groups of children on their way to school, swishing and tapping and knocking their sticks in an unknowing rehearsal of age. Here in Kensington few appeared to be awake before ten in the morning. The mail was delivered late. If there were children they were driven silently to school in large dark cars. I might have felt stranded had I not known that other writers lived in Kensington. I liked to think they were working near, unseen, never forgetting or abandoning the Mirror City.

In the centre of my dining table I put the bowl of planted flowers sent by the Gouldens to welcome me on my first day in the apartment. They had also sent an invitation to their home to meet the author Alan Sillitoe and his wife, Ruth, at afternoon tea, and on the day, in spite of the heavy rain, I chose to walk to their place in Mayfair, planning a route where I might arrive fairly dry. The rain persisted. I did not find the verandahs I had hoped to find. My shoes filled with water, my stockings, the lower part of my dress, the back of my cardigan were soaking when at last I stood outside the Gouldens' apartment and watched the Sillitoes arriving warm and dry by taxi. I was hot, red-faced, flurried; my bladder was full, and my visit was just beginning. I waited 'in the shadows' as it were until the Sillitoes had gone into the building, then I took the lift to the top floor, rang the bell, and was admitted by Mrs Goulden, tall, dark, regal (with a remarkable resemblance, I thought, to the Queen of Spades in the film I had lately seen, *The Manchurian Candidate*). She wore black and had an air of having lived inside her skin as if it were a house, polished, prepared daily, with herself the mistress in total possession. She was not an immediate person; there was a porch, an entrance hall where one waited to be received. She introduced me to Alan and Ruth Sillitoe. ('I've read your books . . . etc.')

The introductions over, there was consternation that my clothes and shoes were saturated. Mrs Goulden took me to a bedroom where she found dry clothes and shoes for me to wear while mine dried, and so I began my visit wearing a tight-fitting black dress and black evening shoes with gold borders, peep toes and two-inch heels.

Presently Mrs Goulden rang a silver bell and a servant, a darkhaired buxom woman named *Columba*, appeared with the afternoon tea and when she had left the room, Mrs Goulden explained that Columba had been brought from Portugal and spoke little English. This caused excitement between the Sillitoes (Alan, the latest star of the northern writers, deep in realism, poverty, struggles for food, work and sex in the slums of the north) had been living in Morocco and had brought a servant home with them, they said, but when they arrived in England, they discovered they had purchased and paid for her as if she were a slave.

Oh, the servant problem!

I listened, quietly amazed, while Mrs Goulden and the Sillitoes ranged from the servant problem to the au pair and back to the servant problem; there in the Mayfair apartment with its Persian rugs, Turkish cats, exquisite paintings, dark knobbly furniture.

I had little to say. I smiled a lot and said 'Yes, yes.' My evening shoes were pinching. And when the time came to leave and I changed into my dry clothes and shoes Mrs Goulden parcelled up the black dress and evening shoes.

'You're welcome to keep them,' she said.

The rain had stopped. No, I said, I'd walk home and not get a taxi. As I left, carrying my new black dress and evening shoes, I thought, with excitement and satisfaction, I have met Alan and Ruth Sillitoe. My second *real* writer. (The first had been John Silkin who had given me a poem inscribed to me, but that is another story.)

Living in South Kensington I could not rid myself of the idea that I was playing house, playing at being someone who lived in an apartment with a white entry phone and a white telephone in the bedroom, beside the bed, for me to answer calls in the middle of the night, 'Oh is that you darling. Don't bother me now.' Playing at having a real bathroom and bath with hot water and cupboards full of linen and huge towels labelled *Bath Sheets* for me to wrap around me when Nigel or Gerald came (opening the door with their private key) and I called, 'Just a minute, *hunny*, I'm in the bath,' with the imagined dialogue the same as that used when I and my sisters played Hollywood with our kewpie dolls. The apartment was a game, beginning with my role as tenant to the unrealistic rent that I would never have money to pay.

And each day I sat at my table trying to write my new novel, *Letter to a Sculptor*. Then I'd get up and walk around the apartment and gloat over it as I used to gloat over the garden in Suffolk, as if producing it had been 'all my own work'. And instead of returning to my typewriter and shaping a batch of sentences, I'd experiment with the new stove in the kitchen, producing an unusual dish from *Aunt Daisy's Recipe Book* sent to me by my father for my last birthday. He'd also sent me a case of New Zealand butter which, after giving some away, I had packed in the snowy refrigerator.

Then one day a friend of Frank Sargeson, Paula Lincoln, who had left New Zealand after thirty years and bought a cottage in a small village in Norfolk, wrote to say that she and her sister Rachel who were ardent cricket fans were coming to London to see the cricket at Lords and they'd like to accept the invitation I had given them to 'stay any time'.

I met them at Liverpool Street Station. They were to sleep in the bedroom while I slept on a folding bed placed half in and out of the hall cupboard with just enough room for passing into the kitchen. I found both Paula and Rachel overwhelming, eager, enthusiastic, moving abruptly in what seemed like a physical attack on the space around them; and as they were sisters who did not see each other often, their voices were high-pitched with excitement and their Oxford accents, sharply edged, sliced through the apartment, furniture, fittings, air and my ears. At Lords I sat watching a tedious game that I knew nothing about, and when a newcomer whispered urgently to me, 'I say, who's first man?' and I echoed meekly, 'First man?' the woman looked at me with disgust.

Halfway through the morning I left Paula and Rachel and returned to Kensington where I found a letter from my sister in New Zealand telling me that my father, cycling to his work as boiler attendant 'out the North Road' had collapsed near Willowglen, our home, and had been admitted to hospital where a diagnosis was not made at once, and the next day he was being x-rayed, still in a state of collapse, when he died. He had been suffering a haemorrhage from a stomach ulcer.

Poor difficult, bullying, loving Dad, I thought, sighing my tears. Later when Paula and Rachel came home from Lords, I told them my news. What could they say? They began to reminisce about their father, a distant man who when they were children had visited them occasionally in the nursery. They remembered his 'twinkling, kindly eyes' and his shyness. They had called him 'Father'. He was a clergyman at a girls' public school, and because he was employed there the Lincoln family was educated there, and, later, they were at school in Switzerland. They had called their mother, 'Mother'. Their parents came rarely to the nursery, they said, and it was their elder sister to whom they looked for guidance and help.

'Poor Mother,' they said. 'Poor Father.'

And they said to each other, 'Do you remember? . . . ' using words and phrases that were of the nineteen twenties and before and that I'd read only in books. Some of the girls at school had fathers who were 'rotters', they cried. 'Rotters and cads. But Father was tophole, wasn't he?'

That evening as I lay in my foldaway bed I thought of Dad alone at Willowglen and I remembered Aunt Polly's criticism of me for going 'overseas' — 'You are single and it's your place to stay home and look after your father.' Poor Dad with his five-shilling postal notes, and his stinking fish-bag, the inside covered with old fish scales, hanging inside the back door, and his trouser clips for his bike hanging on their hook behind the door, and his face wobbling with tears when he said goodbye at the Wellington wharf.

A few days later I had a letter from the lawyer in Oamaru to say that my brother and I were now joint owners of Willowglen and that I had been left all the contents of the home, and would I be returning to New Zealand as I was the sole executor of my father's estate? My father's estate! There were the home and its contents, enough money for the funeral, a small sum of money for my sister, and a bank book containing six shillings and fourpence. The cash for the funeral and the small bequest came from money won a week earlier in a lottery or on a racehorse, otherwise there would have been nothing.

I consulted Dr Cawley whom I still visited regularly. Should I return to New Zealand? A shocked angry letter from my brother said that Willowglen had been locked up and no-one would let him in, and although he was not living at Willowglen, he was hurt by the idea of not being allowed into his old home.

Should I return? Perhaps I had already made up my mind. The opinion was that it might be unwise to live in New Zealand after my past experience there, and that I might even be in danger from the mistaken diagnosis for few there had questioned it, and now that my books were being published there was constant reference to me as 'unbalanced, insane' with a tendency to ally this to my writing and even make it a reason and explanation for my writing. Perhaps I had already made up my mind, for I realized that I wished to return to live and work in New Zealand. Although I was now being referred to as an 'expatriate' writer, my reasons for leaving New Zealand, apart from the desire to 'broaden my experience', had not been literary or artistic. My reason for returning was literary. Europe was so much on the map of the imagination (which is a limitless map, indeed) with room for anyone who cares to find a place there, while the layers of the long dead and recently dead are a fertile growing place for new shoots and buds, yet the prospect of exploring a new country with not so many layers of mapmakers, particularly the country where one first saw daylight and the sun and the dark, was too tantalising to resist. Also, the first layer of imagination mapped by the early inhabitants leaves those who follow an access or passageway to the bone. Living in New Zealand, would be for me, like living in an age of mythmakers; with a freedom of imagination among all the artists because it is possible to begin at the beginning and to know the unformed places and to help to form them, to be a mapmaker for those who will follow nourished by this generation's layers of the dead. I was strongly influenced in my decision by remembering, from time to time, Frank Sargeson's words to me, 'Remember you'll never know another country like that where you spent your earliest years. You'll never be able to write intimately of another country.'

My argument had always been, 'What of the writers forced into political exile who never had or have the choice of returning, who live and work and bring new insights to the language of their adopted country? And what of those who have had to go more deeply into the unknown by changing their language? Conrad, Nabokov . . . and what about James Joyce . . . and Samuel Beckett . . . ? All writers — all beings — are exiles as a matter of course. The certainty about living is that it is a succession of expulsions of whatever carries the life force . . . All writers are exiles wherever they live and their work is a lifelong journey towards the lost land . . . '

The fact is that when I was about to go home to New Zealand I did not need reasons for returning; but others needed to know why, to have explanations. I could have said that, sitting at my sewing machine table looking out at the fields of East Suffolk, I had known a sensation of falseness, of surface-skimming . . . the feeling, perhaps, when after writing a letter and sealing it and writing the address on the envelope one might find that the stamp won't hold, there's nothing to glue it to the envelope, and no matter how hard one tries, the stamp keeps coming unstuck — so what use, except as a self-confirming exercise, was a letter that stayed with the writer?

Whatever my reasons for returning to New Zealand, I knew I would try to make them sound as elevated as possible; but I did experience this unease in Suffolk, knowing that thousands of miles away there was a cabbage tree or a clump of snowgrass or a sweep of sky that I had not examined as carefully as I examined the ninety-foot lilac hedge; and a nation of people that I had never learned to know as well, as during my short stay in Suffolk — or in Ibiza or Andorra — I felt I knew the inhabitants, their landscape, their history and was beginning to know their language.

Now that writing was my only occupation, regardless of the critical and financial outcome, I felt I had found my 'place' at deeper level than any landscape of any country would provide. In New Zealand Frank Sargeson had saved my life by affirming that I could spend my time writing, although to him, I think, I was always the 'mad, sane' person; here in London writing had been affirmed as a way of life without psychiatric qualifications. I now felt, inhabiting my 'place', that day by day I could visit the Mirror City and ponder questions that only those trying to practise a form of art have time for: artists, monks, idlers, any who stand and stare. I could journey like a seasoned traveller to the Mirror City, observing (not always consciously), listening, remembering and forgetting. The only graveyard in Mirror City is the graveyard of memories that are resurrected, reclothed with reflection and change, their essence untouched. (A truthful autobiography tries to record the essence. The renewal and change are part of the material of fiction.)

Having advised against my returning to New Zealand, and accepting that I chose to return, Dr Cawley reminded me that I should live as I wished and not as others wished, that I had no obligation to 'mix', that he agreed with me that living alone was my ideal way of life if I chose it to be. And writing.

He did advise that I buy a return ticket.

I knew, finally, that leaving one's native land forever can be a strength or a weakness or both, depending on the artist, to be used to add to the store of material processed in Mirror City, and that for the writer of fiction being an exile may be a hindrance, especially if the writer is from a country just beginning its literary tradition. The writer (if there is ever such a person as 'the writer') may find herself spending a lifetime looking into the mists of a distant childhood, or becoming a travel writer who describes the scene, then leaves it, pocketing the uprooted vegetation, erasing the sea and the sky without hearing the cries of a world that has been torn from itself into the fictional world, from people whose very skin is left hanging in the centuries-old trees; the unmistakable cry of a homeland truthfully described and transformed.

I know that unless the writer embraces the language of the new land there are constant betrayals of language. (Language may betray the writer but the writer must not be the betrayer.) When I had returned to New Zealand and wrote *The Adaptable Man* set in Suffolk, a sharp-eyed critic noted my inaccurate reference to the *Orwell River* instead of the correct, *River Orwell*, my usage being the New Zealand

153

idiom—the Rakaia River, the Waitaki River, the Clutha River—and not the English—River Thames, Humber, Orwell.

Wherever one lives, in the growing necessity for a 'world view', living or not living in one's native land may give equal advantages and insights, and from whatever land, the truth is always painful to extract and express whether it be the truth of fact or fiction.

I had written a few chapters of *Letters to a Sculptor*. Although my return fare to New Zealand had been guaranteed by 'an anonymous donor' whom I suspected (correctly, I think) to be Charles Brasch (the poet), I preferred to receive money from an institution rather than an individual. I had enough to pay my return fare and my proportion of the rent of the Kensington apartment, but there were no prospects of my being able to have funds in New Zealand. I therefore applied either for a Literary Fund Grant or for the Scholarship in Letters for 1964.

I booked my passage, a single cabin on the *Corinthic*, a one-class ship sailing from London through the Panama Canal to Auckland. I knew I had been advised never again to travel by sea but I was ever hopeful of becoming a good sailor.

Where had my London years gone? Why had I never been to Stratford-on-Avon? To the Brontë country? To Hardy country? Stonehenge, Tintagel Castle, Tintern Abbey? I had spent a week in the Lake District camping out for one night beside Sour Milk Force on the route through to Buttermere. I had roamed the Fells all day visiting places known to Wordsworth, Coleridge, Shelley.

I had absorbed much from living in London. I had seen the rise and strength of the Campaign for Nuclear Disarmament, the Easter Marches to Aldermaston; the Suez crisis; the Hungarian Revolution, the Parliamentary scandals. I had seen the arrival of the 'kitchen sink' playrights and painters, the West Indian novelists, the North Country novelists and I had found my favourites to take their place beside those already there—I read the Beat Poets of City Lights Press; Ted Hughes, Sylvia Plath (recently dead); William Golding; Samuel Selvon; Iris Murdoch, Albert Camus, Sartre, Duras, Sarraute, Robbe-Grillet . . . I had seen *Last Year in Marienbad* and the new films from India. I had attended a performance of *Three Sisters* in Russian . . . I had listened in St Pancras Hall to the London Mozart Players, the Bach Players . . . and Kathleen Ferrier, dead. I had interesting correspondence with Bertrand Russell's first love. The librarian at the Kentish Town flat had sponsored me for a ticket to the British Museum Reading

Room. Well, my London days were full of experience — museum, galleries, libraries, people; and underlying all was a gradual strengthening of me in my place through my talks with Dr Cawley as if he was a *bespoke* tailor helping to reinforce the seams of my life and now I was putting on my own garment to try it. And woven into the garment were my experiences in Ibiza and Andorra. (I'd had a loving postcard from the fur shop in the south of France, from El Vici Mario, but the address was illegible and I therefore excused myself from replying.)

There were many people I knew whom I do not describe here; they are living and I have tried to restrict myself to my own story without presuming to tell the stories of others. Writing of the dead is a different matter, for the dead have surrendered their story. There is a danger, however, in living at a distance from the source of one's fiction, for one so easily equates distance with death, and, rejoicing over the freedom of a story, one is suddenly faced with the curtailing effects of facts that have never undergone the necessary transformation in Mirror City; the writer has supposed that staying safe in this world and sprinkling a potion of distance-death upon a chosen ingredient of fiction, can result in the same transformation that occurs within the harsh lonely places of Mirror City. Instant fiction is as contradictory as instant future.

I said goodbye to London where living had been for me like living within a huge family with London our house. I looked forward to the terrible winters of frost, ice, chilblains. I watched the leaves turning and falling and drifting against the black iron railing of the parks. I saw the sun change to blood-red and stand on end upon the winterbeaten grass of the Common; I watched the people with a new urgency in their gait, hurrying to their homes, if they had homes to escape the dark and the cold; and those with no homes depending for warmth and shelter on the doorways of peopleless places like banks and insurance buildings and (before the great railway stations were demolished or remodelled and rebuilt without seating) on the seats of the railway stations and bus terminals and down from the Strand, by the river, underneath the arches. Then after dark the new life of London, the glitter, the people in taxis and dark polished cars . . . wandering misfits shouting at the sky . . . the dark January days . . . the appearance of spring . . . June, dusty July, August, the cycle again. The seasons in the city of millions became my relations as they had been in the countryside of New Zealand. Here there was the evidence of lives shared with the human power of destruction and creation; the irreparable mistakes that are part of the construction of a city, no matter how carefully it has been planned, the effect of the mistakes, some disastrous, the illumination of the way of human beings, shafts of light not originating in the sun; while the seasons, modified, damaged, but recurring, continue to regard the city, they too in a sense at home, acclimatized to themselves. The effect of London as a vast city gives only a hint of the complexity of Mirror City, yet it filled my life with thoughts and images that have stayed and will stay until I, as a season, accept inevitable change, when leaves of my own memory drift downward to become part of the rich earth of Mirror City.

My departure from London was sad and strange. With scenes in my mind of my journey from New Zealand, of my father, Uncle Vere and Aunty Polly waving goodbye from the shelter of the wharf sheds in Wellington; streamers, the ritual playing of *Now is the Hour*, the fearful apprehension that came over me when I watched the hills receding, the rising sense of adventure when I realized there was no turning back. I tried to imagine how it would be now, leaving London. The wharf, the embarkation, sailing down the Thames to the open sea . . . but where were the people to say goodbye in a city where my only family was the city itself?

I had spent seven years away from New Zealand with my past few years occupied entirely with writing, dividing my time between writing, solitary walking, dreaming in cinemas. I had no close friends who might wish to stand on a London wharf waving a sad goodbye. Unable to face a solitary departure I asked the librarian who had secured me a ticket to the Reading Room, would she mind 'seeing me off'. She agreed. The literary agent, Patience Ross, farewelled me at Victoria Station, and when the train arrived at the East London docks there was Millicent the librarian, who had taken an extended lunch hour to say goodbye. We had afternoon tea on board ship. I thanked her. She returned to her work. And as the engines started and the last farewells were made, and the ship began to move down the Thames, I looked about me at the sober, subdued passengers. There had been no band playing, no streamers. Some of the passengers had the air of being about to sail to their doom; many, no doubt were emigrants who had said last goodbyes and would never return; faces showed anxiety rather than anticipation, a certainty of a journey away from rather than a journey towards.

Recovering from my own brief self-pity (all those years in London and I need to ask someone to say goodbye to me!) I looked with interest at the dock buildings and the dark dampness of 'dockside' and I thought of my father and his Sexton Blake paperbacks, half-sized pocketbooks on mottled paper, and their scenes of crime in London's dockland; and the character, Tinker's, 'Right, guv.' I thought how much Dad would have relished a description of the docks, and how grateful he would have been, like one who feels the movement of a telephone wire although there is no distinct message, had I written to say that I could just imagine Tinker and Sexton Blake at the docks meeting some unsavoury character, a 'nark' who would give them the 'tip-off'.

And so it was not the buildings of London, the Tate Gallery, the new literature, the excitement of living in London, that I thought of as the ship sailed towards the open sea, it was the girlhood sharing with my father of the cheap, poorly-written detective stories with their pulp-soaked racist stereotypes, Tinker and Sexton Blake and their 'guvs' and 'm'lords' and 'm'luds' who were yet fictional characters whatever their literary deficiencies; and it was not even Dickens or Lamb or Samuel Pepys, it was Sexton Blake and Tinker, his faithful servant, who farewelled me from London while I, in my turn, was waving goodbye for the last time to my father, he too perhaps sheltering in fiction, huddled by the docks in the company of Tinker and Sexton Blake of Baker Street.

The
Return

22

The seasickness that began as soon as we pitched and rolled on the open sea did not appear so hopeless from a deck cabin with a fresh breeze blowing in or from a deckchair outside. I was sitting quietly in a deckchair, trying to work out a way of having meals and avoiding the terrible weakness when a young man came out on deck.

'Would you like a slice of my birthday cake?' he asked. 'My mother made it for me.'

'Oh thank you.' I said. We were now two days out of London and I'd had no food, except the biscuits I'd brought with me.

The young man sat beside me. His name was Albert, he said, and he was a nuclear physicist travelling to take up a post in a New Zealand university where he hoped to concentrate on geophysics, volcanoes and earthquakes.

He was a mild, shy, pale young man in his late twenties, and from that day whenever I took up my place in the deckchair outside my cabin, sooner or later he would appear, sit beside me and talk to me. He brought me food from the dining room, and it was not long before he was bringing a small meal on a tray, enough for me to survive without increasing the sickness by making the journey to the dining room in the depths of the ship.

I told him I was a writer returning home after seven years away, but when he asked about the titles of my books my almost primitive shyness about naming prevented me from telling him. If, as is often said, the role of a poet is to name, then I understand my diffidence in naming titles, my reluctance to reduce or drain into speech the power supply of the named.

Albert became my attendant and companion throughout the voyage. His conversation was interesting. He was curious about the nature of the world, and I was an eager listener. He had spent his life asking questions and answering some of them. It is dismal to be alone and ill on land but the misery increases on board ship if one can't walk to the dining room to eat the meals enticingly displayed in the shipping brochure, nor see the films, nor take part in the games or the dancing, but can only lounge in a deckchair and not even travel into a poem or dream. Albert, full of information, brought news of life on board ship and of the world of science. I remembered how in my university days when I pored over the university calendars reading the science curriculum, I felt the excitement and mystery of the subject, 'Heat, Light and Sound', and I thought, 'Surely this is the province of poets, painters, composers of music, as well as of scientists, and why is it reserved exclusively for a handful of students?' And I remembered how, lured by the mystery and the magic, I borrowed books on physics and, opening them, I was faced with a wall of figures and symbols far beyond my Scholarship mathematics and chemistry: sentences that I could not understand, that roused the same feeling of frustration I'd had when I tried to read my father's bagpipe music as if it were simply another book, and it *was* a book. How could Heat, Light, Sound belonging to everyone, so remove itself from us? And I felt the frustration of the limits of my mind, curiosity and eagerness turning to dull fury and a surrender to myself as myself and not as I dreamed I might be, because I, living always with heat, light, sound, was excluded from its secrets.

It was thus a rare gift for me to have for thirty-one days the company of a 'real' physicist, this quiet shy man, a member of the Society of Friends, a great nephew of a famous poet, a pacifist and campaigner for nuclear disarmament who had worked at an atomic station and whose life was the study of violent earth movements, upheavals of fire and ashes, and whose recent invention had been a *safety detonator*: like his subject, Heat, Light, Sound, he was a living contradiction.

When the ship berthed at various ports my seasickness disappeared as soon as the ship stopped moving, and Albert and I went ashore and I listened eagerly while he described the formations of earth, water, sky, and asked and answered How, What, Where. And at the end of the voyage I felt that Albert's presence on board ship, through luck, coincidence or mysterious providence, had enabled me to survive.

At last we entered the Hauraki Gulf sailing slowly past the Bays with their unexpectedly colourful houses like rows of boiled sweets (ten years earlier I would have said 'lollies') in pink, yellow, blue, green, with some striped—set against the vivid green grass (leaf green? veridian?) and the darker green where stands of native bush remained. I'd forgotten about the confectionery housepaint and the drowning depths of the blue sky, not distant, but at hand, at head, a shared sky.

'Isn't Auckland pretty?' someone said.

'Isn't it?'

And there again was the Auckland light, not forgotten, like mountain light in a city without mountains, yet softer, full of currents of buoyant blue and purple and grey, and, moving, one waded effortlessly through the light.

When the Customs and Health launch arrived, members of the press also came on board, and I was surprised that they asked to talk to me. I had not realized that in the seven years I had been absent, the publication overseas and in New Zealand of several books had built a reputation known as an *overseas reputation* and therefore valued apparently more than a reputation *within New Zealand*—the reputation of excellent writers living in New Zealand was usually qualified by the phrase *known within New Zealand only*. (The growth of jet planes and the building of airports known as *international* resulted in the decline of *overseas* as an adjective of prestige and its replacement with *international*—an *international reputation*.) Also, as I'd been absent there had been no visible person to fasten this reputation upon, and with my arrival home, a dam of opinion and speculation burst over me. I had been quite unaware of this. I came home to find that I was looked on, variously, as famous, rich, a woman of the world, sane, insane, inevitably different from the shy unknown who had departed. Had I not lived and worked *overseas*? Had not my books been noticed *overseas*? Why, I was asked, as if there were no possible reason, should I want to return to New Zealand?

Perhaps we are a lazy people; the literary world is lazy too, preferring to pick up reputations from overseas rather than risk their own judgment within New Zealand.

The ship berthed. Albert's former colleague at the atomic station who had promised to meet him had sent his daughter. Her father was dying of cancer, she said. I wondered about the atomic station and its safety, for other colleagues had died.

My sister, her husband and children met me and drove me across the new Harbour Bridge ('see, there's our Harbour Bridge') to Northcote where they had hired a small caravan for me to stay until I travelled south to Oamaru and Willowglen. Where the Gordons had once lived surrounded by bush with tall kauris there were now rows of houses and acres of concrete, while the once wet wooded roadsides were treeless. The Gordon children, now teenagers, with Pamela at Intermediate School, filled the tiny house as they took up their places to watch *Ponderosa* or *Wagon Train* on television.

Later when I began to walk to Frank Sargeson's place in Esmonde Road, I discovered that except for a stand at Northcote by the harbour, all the bush had vanished and the country road to Takapuna where cows, horses, swamphens had once stared at the solitary walker, now was lined on each side by a ribbon of houses from Northcote to Takapuna, while the end of Frank's road, once secluded with mangroves, swamp, sea, had been extended, the swamp filled in, the land 'reclaimed', and the approach road to the Harbour Bridge built upon it. Suddenly thrust into a world where there was much talk of 'reclaimed' land, 'desirable' property, the price of sections, sections with and without views, I felt I was seeing a new kind of greed for whatever could be touched, measured, seen, and priced. I was in a new city that looked outward and hoped and prayed for and paid for a *view*. And no-one was saying what or whom the land belonged to before the famous reclamation.

Frank's bach had been almost surrounded by 'units' built upon what was now expensive 'real estate'. I felt sad as I bent forward to clear the evergrowing hedge with the honeysuckle as its sweet parasite, and trod the path that was now set with concrete paving stones, like stepping stones from one world to another, towards the back door with its empty upturned jar clamped upon the familiar message scribbled on the scrap of green paper. *Janet. Back at three-thirty*. With a cross for a kiss.

I pushed open the door. I felt very much like the Traveller returning.

161

The bulk of manuscripts and books had increased while a huge bookcase (recognized as once belonging to the aunts who had died) divided the corner bed from the kitchen counter. There was a new large wooden chair used like a deckchair, the back adjusting with a wooden rod into several reclining positions. A writing-board, a pile of ink-written manuscripts upon it, was set beside another wooden chair by the counter. The rows of fruit, groups of peppers, seeds, were still there along the windowsill and on the counter. The circle of damp in the pinex ceiling had spread, still in a circle, with scalloped edges. The wood of the counter, the built-in desk (its surface covered with books), the chairs, the mantelpiece, the door, the bed-base, the windowsills and frames, had a more mellowed, worn appearance as if each day had passed across the surface, leaning on and fingering and even striking blows on the now golden wood.

I heard the swish of the overgrown vegetation as Frank came around the corner of the bach. I sensed that he was as apprehensive as I about our meeting after seven years. I could see his nervousness, but when we saw each other we each knew we were as we had been in that we were recognizable to each other after seven years. The tension eased.

Frank, preparing a cup of tea behind the counter, said hurriedly, 'You know, I'm not jealous. I'm not jealous.'

I was surprised that he, too, had been trapped by the words 'overseas reputation', and that he had expected to see someone different from the scared J. F. who stayed in the hut seven years ago.

Then, 'Have you seen it?' he asked.

'Seen what?'

'The hut. I had to have it demolished. It was overrun with rats and falling to pieces. You don't have to see it if you don't want to. I know it will distress you.'

I was touched by Frank's everlasting concern, and I felt ashamed of my lack of feeling for the hut. We went down the overgrown garden ('that's all gone,' he said sadly) by the tall flourishing pawpaw tree, its already gnarled trunk and twisted branches recording experience of direction, time, weather, unknown to the stripling new tree I had last seen in Frank's garden. We came to the heap of rubble that had been the hut where I lived and wrote, and now it was hidden by grass, paspalum and wild-seeded sweetcorn. I could see the burned circle of earth where I used to destroy all but the last version of manuscripts. I felt no regret, although careful of Frank's feelings and expectations, I sighed. 'Well, it's sad,' I said, and I felt sad then, but I knew that although I had lost the hut when I left Takapuna, I had kept within myself the memory of the time I spent there, knowing it was one of the cherished times of my life: the material vanishing now was nothing.

Frank then showed me the room he'd had built for Harry, with its separate entrance a grape arbour where already the white grapes hung in clusters.

'Taste them,' he said, tugging at a laden stalk. 'I give them to the paperboy.'

They were small, hard, bitter.

Frank then cooked a meal while he gave news of our friends, acquaintances, visitors, and the bodgies and widgies who had invaded his bach.

'And Karl and Kay Stead?'

He gave their news.

'Maurice and Barbara Duggan?'

'Jess and Ernest Whitworth? Jack? Harry? Reece Cole and Christine? Tony Stones? Kevin Ireland? Ian Hamilton? Werner and Greville? Odo Strewe? That small dark woman, you remember she came here only once and you said that if you'd ever been the marrying kind you would have married her?'

'Mrs Ansell?'

He gave news of her. He had news of everyone. Bob Lowry, Glover, Curnow, Shadbolt, Nigel Cook, Jimmy, Clarrie, Ted Middleton, Dennis McEldowney . . . everyone. Frank Haig? . . . on and on.

'And Charles Brasch?'

He gave all news, out-of-town and Auckland news, the out-of-town news having suffered a certain dilution, especially if it had crossed Cook Strait. He told of the new writers, too, many of them. 'You may have an international reputation,' he said, 'but do you know, Janet, you and I are *passé*.'

I thought that perhaps he was right.

In my memory I hold this sheaf of pages labelled *The Return*; some pages are faded, some still starkly printed. When Frank asked where I would be living, saying there was always a bed for me at 14 Esmonde Road, I told him of my application for the Scholarship in Letters for 1964. I'd be returning to Willowglen, I said, to tidy affairs there, then I'd find a room in Auckland or the North Shore to live and write. In the meantime I had use of the eight-foot caravan at my sister's place in Northcote.

The visit to Willowglen was urgent. My brother had written that the house had been broken into several times: the new pair of double blankets had been stolen, he said. Other possessions were missing. I could feel the intensity underlining the reference to household goods and I knew with the wonder of recognition that I still had my passport to Mirror City, that it was my true home no matter how small my talent might be, how clumsy my sentences; each day and night I was in touch with the unalterable human composition that is the true basis of fiction, the great events of everyone's life and death — the returns, the losses, the gains, and now, anticipating my visit to my old home, the long pursuit of and flight from the dead and the goods of the dead. The news that the Kaiapoi blankets, soft white woollen blankets never known but now precious, had gone or been stolen, encompassed a cry to bring back the dead.

The next day I booked my seat on the overnight train to Wellington and the express across the Canterbury plains and the salmon river, to Oamaru.

Willowglen

23

Arriving in Oamaru, I went at once to the motor camp where I had rented a unit for the night. I bought supplies from the dairy and I stared curiously at the dairy owner, Mr Grant, who had been named next-of-kin when my father collapsed outside the shop. I looked searchingly at the goods I bought as if they and Mr Grant and my father were now in possession of a death I had come too late to share.

When I walked back to my cabin I saw a young man hiding in the bushes and peering out at me. He came towards me. He was a reporter, he said, from the local newspaper and he hoped I would give him first chance to talk to me as the provincial paper was also looking for me. He too had been fed the diet of 'overseas reputation' causing him to form an unreal image of me. He'd been sent to find the New Zealand author who was now jewelled with *overseas*, to gaze on her and share the jewels; and I, in my paste glitter, felt embarrassed. Although the reporter soon discovered that I did not carry the riches he expected, he was pleased to be first with his story, *Oamaru Author Returns*. We walked in the Gardens where he photographed me sitting in the Japanese garden, and I was remembering how as children wearing our Aunty-Polly-made puffed-sleeve summer-breeze dresses, we had been photographed or 'snapped' near the same bridge.

That day also, I collected the Willowglen key from the lawyer who asked what my plans were for Willowglen. My brother was getting married and needed a home, he said. The place was worth little, he was sure no-one would buy it, and so there was little prospect of a division of money from any sale. He advised me to sell my share and not give it away as I had suggested. My father had wanted me to have it, he said. I had already made up my mind to give my brother my share for I knew he had little money and I also knew that throughout his life he had not been as lucky as I.

First, however, I must visit Willowglen in its springtime. Oamaru, as much as ever the kingdom by the sea, had now been declared a city as its population was up to ten thousand, but it was the sea that still clamoured to be heard, making the city like a shell singing in everyone's ears. My return alone to the deserted Willowglen was softened by the green of the leafy trees, and the sight of the once slender pine trees 'down on the flat', startling at first, as they were now a dark forest almost as formidable as the 'second planny' on the hill of Eden Street, and by the sound of the distant roar of the surf pounding at the breakwater on the shore. The driveway of Willowglen was overgrown with cocksfoot and littered with rusting parts of old cars, old stoves, and remnants of a dray. The shed where the pictures and the heavier furniture had been stored after the move from Eden Street was collapsed upon itself, open to the sky, with picture frames and table-legs still angled among the ruins. The cowbyre, the fowlhouse, the old pigsty overgrown with hemlock, the apple shed were all gradually falling apart, boards hanging, swinging to and fro as if the months and years had passed with such violence as to rip them apart like useless limbs. A wild black cat, perhaps one of Siggie's families, lurked in the hawthorn hedge. Siggie had recently died, aged eighteen.

I walked up the path under the old 'ghost' tree, that huge pine with the drooping dark branches. I walked in the porch, the lean-to against the hill, treading on last year's squashed pears and seeing even among the pear blossom a few, shrivelled and shrunken, still clinging to the tree with no-one to gather them any more. The old iron boot-last was still there, just outside the back door; Dad's fishing bag, as I remembered it in Kensington, fishy-stink and scabbed inside with old dried fish scales; and there were his thigh gumboots for wading in the shingle beds of the Waitaki, Rakaia, Rangitata. I opened the back door and walked in. I had not expected it would be as I found it, yet how else could it have been? My father's pyjamas hung over a chair. His long cream-coloured Mosgiel underpants with a faint brown stain at the crotch lay on the floor; even his last cup of tea sat in its saucer, a swill of tea in the bottom of the cup, making an old brown ridge against the china. The latest—two-and-a-half-months'-old—newspaper folded to present the crossword half filled in with the stub of the ink pencil beside it, lay by the cup of tea. There were ashes in the kitchen range with the ashpan half drawn out ready for emptying, while above, on the brass rack, neatly folded pyjamas lay ready for the night.

The old sofa where Tittups the cat had peed and we tried to absorb the smell with our Christmas carnation scent, where the headmistress of Waitaki sat the day she came to give her sympathy over my sister Isabel's drowning, still took the length of the wall facing the shadowing hill beyond the lean-to where the bank was thick with cocksfoot, periwinkle, and small broadleaf plants sheltering in their own clay bed beneath the parent tree.

In the kitchen, the curtains were new, a bright pattern of teapots and cups and saucers, the kind of pattern mother would never have chosen. I drew aside the curtains by 'Dad's seat' and looked out along the path to the cypress tree and the old dunny with its dunny roses spilling in a mass of white buds over the corrugated tin-hat roof.

I walked into the middle bedroom where I hoped to sleep. Books, linen were scattered everywhere. The two front rooms were also strewn with books, newspapers, old clothes, with the room that used to belong to our parents appearing tidier. There, the bed had some bedclothes and the pink eiderdown bought years ago on account from Calder Mackay, and there was a strange-looking electric heater like a copper pipe in front of the disused fireplace. I opened the front door and looked out at the grassy slope to the old orchard, the creek, and part of the 'flat' where my brother had transported an old house and where, I'd been told, Uncle Charlie, Dad's youngest brother, lived from time to time. I stood at the front door. The grass was growing on the doorstep. I remembered the time the cow had come to the front door and looked in. An owl in the tall macrocarpa tree by the old wash-house, startled by a human presence, fluttered from its sleeping perch to the paddock beyond.

My homecoming was as sad and desolate as I knew it would be, yet I relished its importance to the Envoy from Mirror City, that watching self, who was already waiting to guide me to my fictional home. Many times in my life I have received and cherished these gifts of fiction. From my home now in Mirror City I can only keep trying to parcel these gifts in language that satisfies the ear and the heart and the demands of truth. (It is the events of living that are not easily recognized as legends and part of myths that are the test of the value of lifelong tenancy in Mirror City; and it is the discovery of the new legends and myths that keeps building, renewing the city.)

As I explored the house I realized that I had forgotten or never knew about practical matters like turning on electricity, water, arranging a telephone, and I was reduced at once from the glory of my 'overseas reputation' when I received a bill for having the water switched on, and I was questioned by the power board about my ability to pay. I had forgotten in the midst of apparent kindness shown to me on my return home, that the world is still a cruel place, and Oamaru was no exception, and in all the abundance of Oamaru's giving and taking through water — the reservoir, the sea, the baths, the loved creeks and ponds, even the water-race known to us as the 'rolldown sea' by the post office, everything and everyone must be paid for.

I built a fire down on the flat to burn the rubbish collected in the house — old newspapers, receipts going back many years. I read everything before I burned or saved it. I burned family letters. I saved documents that I thought might be wanted by my sister and brother or myself, some that might be looked on as keepsakes — Isabel's athletic and academic certificates, her funeral receipt, other receipts that still bore the anguish of receiving the account so vividly that I said to myself, I remember when that bill came and Mum cried wondering how we could possibly pay it, but now it's paid and gone; how could a sheet of paper headed 'Dr To' (we had always thought of it as *Doctor*) cause so much anguish? I found the Star-Bowkett Building Society book with its detailed payments on the loan that bought Willowglen, and I heard again the anxiety in Mum's or Dad's voice — 'Where's the Star-Bowkett book? Have we paid the Star-Bowkett this month? When we pay the *Star-Bowkett* . . . ' There were the Calder Mackay receipts, too, everything paid. And the local receipts — MacDiarmids, Bulleids, the Polytechnic, Hodges, Kerrs, Jeffrey and Smith, Adams . . . all the tradespeople that inhabited without knowing it our house, our daily conversation, and determined the mood of the family.

I found a pile of letters in a handwriting I did not recognize, and

I began to read. The letters were from Dad's woman friend living in another town. I had only recently heard about her from my sister who had said they planned to marry. The new curtains and pillowcases had been bought by her. She and Dad had been good company for each other, for apparently she had stayed often at Willowglen and attended to various household chores, and they had enjoyed themselves over a few drinks, as the numerous empty bottles disclosed. Her letters expressed concern over the house and its furnishings. She also wrote of the presents my father had given her, some of which she asked for in her letters.

As I read, I found myself slowly assuming the role of my mother, feeling the shock of knowing that 'Curly' who never 'touched a drop of drink' had left *empty liquor bottles* in the house, that the love that so steadfastly bound him over the years had been cast aside for this 'cheap' relationship with someone obviously in search of a 'sugar daddy'. I then became the outraged daughter — how dare our father abandon us for this woman? How dare she try to replace our mother! And why had Dad never told me? Not a word in all his letters with their detailed times, dates, costs, journeys, and the state of the government. I suddenly felt lonely, an outsider in my family.

Then as the last of the letters flared and died in the ashes I saw my father as he had been — widowed, living alone, troubled by bouts of undiagnosed sickness, still dosing himself with his 'chalk' to ease the pains in his stomach, coping with the physical effort of cycling each day along that bleak sea-exposed road out past the Boys' High to attend the boiler at the Presbyterian Home, returning wearily to an unlit cold house that escaped from the shadow of the hill only twice during the day, in the early morning when the sun trod briefly on the front doorstep and glanced in the window of the side bedroom, and later when it lay a hand along the front windowsill, then withdrew it, disappearing behind the trees. The frost in that all-day shade was as cruel as ever; and even the glorious seafoam wave of pear blossom at the back door could not atone for the awful chill lying all winter outside and inside the draughty, flimsy wooden house.

I prepared the middle bedroom for myself. I lifted the mattress from the floor and found a gaping hole in the cover and, snuggled within the kapok, a nest of bald pink baby rats. I don't recall how I disposed of them.

I washed the available bed linen and hung it to dry on the wire clothesline that stretched from the top of the hill to the apple shed on the flat. I hoisted the line further in the air with the old manuka-stick prop and heard the familiar squeak-squeak as the stretched line pulled at the tree support, the old oak by the apple shed near where mother used to rest before she 'tackled' the steep sloping path to the house. I saw again in my mind my father's hunched figure, the sugar sack of railway coal on his back, his knees bent to ease the strain as he too struggled up the slope that became steeper year by year.

And that night with the house cleaned and the bedclothes dried, I slept in the middle room. I was wakened by the wind in the many trees, by the silence, by the searchlight glare of the midnight express train as it turned the corner past the Gardens towards the railway crossing. The trees heaved and rocked in the rising wind; moreporks and the little 'German' owls called from the macrocarpa. And in the morning I was wakened by the gurgling, gargling magpies.

I decided I would not stay at Willowglen. I would walk into town that morning to book my return passage to Auckland, and when I had chosen those possessions I thought of as 'keepsakes' for members of the family, I would leave Oamaru.

Although the retraced path is a factual and fictional cliché, I'm not beyond indulging my memory. It was a delight to walk down Chelmer Street to the town while remembering other, not happier, times. Chelmer Street, too, with the hilly side of the street facing north, lived in perpetual shade on the north side, with occasional rays of afternoon sun touching the 'Gardens' side of the street. The street was so clearly divided in its share of sun and shade that it was like a street that had suffered a stroke and was left paralysed on one side, with the shade and the frost as the paralysing agents.

At the end of the street I passed the Town Baths and felt again, held within the dull red colour of the rows of seats and their spindly uncomfortable slats, the sense of the old glory of 'being at the Baths', and then I remembered after my sister Myrtle's drowning, the deliberate disentangling, the excision of the baths from my life and the way I then looked on the site as a strange hateful place as if it had been a friendly neighbour who was now an enemy sitting there unpunished for its crime. Now, remembering the succession of feelings towards the Baths, I felt only the sadness of the dull red colour of the seats, that iron-roof, railway-hut, railway-wagon, railway-station red that was painted through my life as part of my childhood rainbow.

I walked through Takaro Park where the circus used to pitch its tent and the sixpenny zoo was held in a row of cages under separate canvas; and there was the old building we used to call the Middle School, used for teaching technical subjects, and always apparently empty during the day. I remembered how I used to walk past it and feel a shiver of curiosity and strangeness at its emptiness and brownness and the tall windows with their cords hanging untouched during the daytime; it was a neutral kind of school, it had fairness, it was middle ground, between the fierce rivalries of the North and the South Schools. I walked by the Oamaru Creek and what I still thought of as the 'Morgue', that small stone hut; and by the green water-race that reminded me of a *weir*, of Maggie Tulliver and *The Mill on the Floss*.

And as I stood in the queue at the post office people spoke to me, welcoming me home to Oamaru; some I knew, others were strangers who had seen my photo in the paper. One woman said she'd been at Waitaki when I was there. I stared at her. 'Oh yes,' and the former rigid classifications came to mind — good at maths; stodgy; not much good at phys. ed. Lives in the country, on a sheep station with a fancy name. Teachers talk with deference of the sheep station. We all turn our heads, envious.

We talked a while. She gave me news of others in the school class. 'Oh? That's interesting, I didn't know. Yes. Oh.'

I walked by the small telegraphic office next to the post office and there was the Social Security Department, and now I remembered my horror and shame as I used to sneak in to present my medical certificate with its telltale writing, *Schizophrenia*, and cash my sickness benefit during my brief stays in Oamaru. I remembered how I used to emerge from that office feeling as if all delight had gone from the day, knowing that I was a 'funny' peculiar person, and wanting to hide forever. I felt dirty, my clothes felt like the clothes of a mental patient, and my shoes looked clumsy.

I allowed myself the luxury of remembering these feelings and knowing that in the magic language of the world of racing — *this time* — everything was different. I need not go to the Social Security Department where the man behind the grille peered at me to see if my schizophrenia were showing.

I returned to Willowglen walking through the Town Gardens with its *Oamaru Beautifying Society* plaques. I passed the fern house and saw the ferns with their hair leaning against the milky windows, and I thought of how as children we used to go to the fern house just to feel the experience of wetness and greenness and the smell of being in the earth with the world above and around. I walked from the

171

Gardens, past Lovers' Lane, the hideaway walk with its tree-enclosed paths, past the children's playground with its seesaws and boat swings and merry-go-round that used to make me so sick I could never play on them. And there was the paddling pool and the murky pond where the ducks and the swans lived, the big white swan with the orange beak and the fierce hooded eyes, and I remembered how I used to think of the Seven Brothers who were changed into swans but there was not enough magic for the youngest who had only one wing and could not fly. And I'd always thought that magic was magic, without limit.

Later that day I searched for keepsakes. I sat among the strewn books that were family books, history books bought by my brother who was always interested in history, 'rogue' books from nowhere, prizes from Waitaki. I chose my sister Isabel's school prizes, Christmas books, London, my Training College *David Copperfield* and school prizes; Isabel's collection of native plants. For June and her family, Dad's book of fishing flies, the polished rod and case won in a fishing competition and never used because he preferred to make his own; various books; dishes, table covers, and the old kitchen clock with the dragons around the glass face. For myself, a pair of old blankets, the eiderdown, Dad's paintings, leaving some for my brother, Aunty Polly and Aunty Isy's paintings, the bagpipe chanter, the bedcover sewn by Dad from the collection of blazer material from throughout New Zealand, used by Aunty Isy at the Ross and Glendining Mills. There was little more that I could take in my luggage. I had no place of my own to live in. My brother could make good use of the rest of the family 'treasures'.

Sitting there choosing and rejecting from the pathetic remnants of a family's life, I could still feel the value of them, my need for them, the need of others to have them as keepsakes. Each object was alive with its yesterdays. I wanted to embrace them, even the books; and when I finally packed them, I looked regretfully at those I had been forced to leave behind: the long kauri form where we used to sit for meals and where my father and his brothers and sisters had also sat, and, like us, had used the upturned form as a canoe. The dining table had been used only on special occasions at Eden Street, but at Willowglen it would fit only into the small kitchen: it had been the Christmas and New Year table, the Sunday Bible-reading table, the table-when-visitors-came; Dad's leather workbag which he always sewed while we watched fascinated as he trimmed the raw leather, cut the bag to shape, stained it, and finally sewed it, first drawing the thread through a lump of beeswax. I pocketed a few of his salmon spoons and sinkers only because we had shared, too, in their making, watching (seen and not heard) while Dad leaned over the stove with the sinkers in their small pan, and the dreaded 'spirits of salts'.

Having a last look over the house I opened the sewing machine drawer where the bullets used to be kept and there they were, two or three, shining with a point at the end like bronzed rockets. 'Don't you touch the bullets,' our parents would say. Curious, we often touched them, and played school with them, marshalling them along the mottled brown varnished machine-stand.

And so with my bundle of treasures from Willowglen I took the train and ferry north to Auckland.

Only
to
Please
the Envoy

24

Treasures dreamed of and seen in their own home are different when they are homeless. I arrived at the Gordon's place in Northcote with a heap of apparent rubbish — a bundle of frayed linen, an old broken kitchen clock, a chipped ivory chanter without a reed, a stained flybook that clearly wanted to be in no other place but clasped in my father's hand or thrust like a wallet in the outer pocket of his fishing bag; a golden cut glass dish where mother used to make the Christmas and New Year jellies that we would hold up to the light and look through, to see the gold; a small dark blue china shoe that used to be on the mantelpiece at home and held an assortment of needles, buttons, clips. The only item of worth was the unused fishing rod in its new varnished case, and the red fan heater. In the Gordon's smart new house ('designed by an architect') with its 'cedar weatherboards' and 'cantilever terrace' and 'peep of Rangitoto', the treasures looked pathetic. Except for the cut glass dish, the china shoes, and the heater (which with the bedcover of blazer cloth I gave to Frank Sargeson), they were thrust under the house by the garage where one of my suitcases of possessions had been left while I was away overseas. Returning, opening the mouldy case, I had felt the fumes of past misery rising from the dark blue and dark green remnants of skirts and jerseys, the everglaze summer dress (again dark blue with pattern of exploding stars), the typed pages of old poems and stories wedged into a ravine of yesterdays.

The kitchen clock with the dragons on the glass, the old bedcovers lay homeless among the bits and pieces until one or two found a place in the playhouse of my niece, Pamela, where they revived, briefly at home among fantasy teas and conversations. I remember my anger and shock when I perceived that the treasures I had rescued were being treated carelessly, ill used, not given their pride of place; and then I smiled to myself at my concern as I realized that even in my journeys to Mirror City I had abducted treasures from their homeland, placed them in strange settings, changed their purpose, and in some cases destroyed them to make my own treasures even as my niece was doing in her playhouse. And here was I being trapped also within one of the great themes of fiction — the gift, the giver, the receiver and the thing received, a theme so basic it is embedded in the grammar and syntax of the language where it lies like a trap or a shaft of light.

In writing this autobiography I have been returning to each year of my life to collect the treasures of my experience, and I have set them down in their own home, their own place. In my record I have returned to New Zealand where I am awarded the Scholarship in Letters for 1964 that enables me to write without financial worry for a year, and in 1965 I become a Burns Fellow at the University of Otago where I can buy a cottage for twelve hundred pounds . . . my writing continues, living and expressing. In trying to secure and bring home to their place the treasures of my recent past I find that, like Pamela with her playhouse of fantasy, carpeting her floor with old treasures, pouring her teas out of cups and saucers removed from their home but transformed in their new setting, I prefer to take my treasures to my home, my playhouse, Mirror City. I have the pressure of the Envoy to do this, and even as I write now the Envoy from Mirror City waits at my door, and watches hungrily as I continue to collect the facts of my life. And I submit to the Envoy's wishes. I know that the continued existence of Mirror City depends on the substance transported there, that the waiting Envoy asks, 'Do you wish Mirror City to thrive? Remember your visit there, that wonderful view over all time and space, the transformation of ordinary facts and ideas into a shining palace of mirrors? What does it matter that often as you

175

have departed from Mirror City bearing your new, imagined treasures, they have faded in the light of this world, in their medium of language they have acquired imperfections you never intended for them, they have lost meaning that seemed, once, to shine from them and make your heart beat faster with the joy of discovery of the matched phrase or cadence, the clear insight. Take care. Your recent past surrounds you, has not yet been transformed. Do not remove yet what may be the foundation of a palace in Mirror City.'

I plead, 'Let me write of further travel, of the way of life of a writer in New Zealand, of my return to Dunedin and the University, of books written and books planned, of friends made and kept. Quick, just once, let me look out at the clouds travelling along the North-East Valley sky in Dunedin, that immense sky sprawled above the hills, with every cloud going somewhere in a trail of white or black smoke pursued by storm and wind and sun. And let me describe how . . . '

'There is much to do,' the Envoy says, looking over my shoulder as I see in my mind the clouds in the Dunedin sky. 'And what is that city shining across the valley?' the Envoy asks.

I look triumphant.

'That's Dunedin. I was born there. Let me write of my life there, how I made friends and wrote books, how I went north to live by the sea, how I moved to other cities with other clouds and skies.'

'You say it's Dunedin? It's Mirror City. You know it's time to pack this collection of years for your journey to Mirror City.'

I stare more closely at the city in my mind. And why, it *is* Mirror City, it's not Dunedin or London or Ibiza or Auckland or any other cities I have known. It is Mirror City before my own eyes. And the Envoy waits.